M000290004

ROLEX GOLD

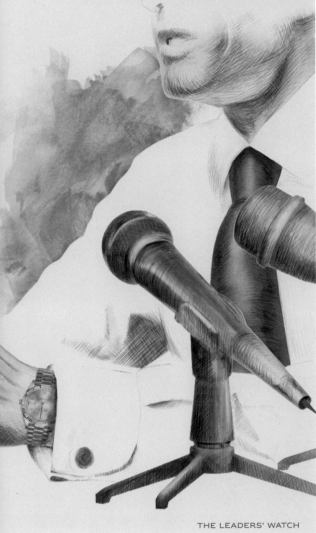

THE LEADERS' WATCH

IS A WITNESS TO THOSE WHO CHANGE THE WORLD.

Chosen by presidents, world leaders and visionaries since 1956, the Day-Date was the first watch to display the date and day in full. With the new Day-Date 40, Rolex redefines watchmaking once again. Built the Rolex Way, it is equipped with calibre 3255, Rolex's all-new movement with 14 patents that sets a new standard in mechanical performance. Available exclusively in platinum or 18 ct gold, the Day-Date is the international icon of achievement and success. It doesn't just tell time. It tells history.

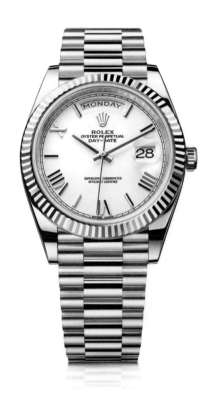

OYSTER PERPETUAL DAY-DATE 40

ROLEX

NEW
PERSPECTIVES
ON SCANDINAVIAN
DESIGN

MUUTO

Frame: MYKITA DECADES SUN GINA | Photography: Mark Borthwick

MYKITA

BERLIN | CARTAGENA | COPENHAGEN | LOS ANGELES | MONTERREY
NEW YORK | PARIS | TOKYO | VIENNA | WASHINGTON | ZERMATT | ZURICH

SHOP ONLINE AT MYKITA.COM

Photography by Jeremy Coysten

Produced at Stoneywood paper mill, Scotland.
Made to exacting standards since 1888,
Conqueror is internationally recognised as the superior
choice for business and creative communications.

It is the fine paper of designers and artists,
and the stationery paper of royalty and statesmen.

Introducing Conqueror Feather, Pencil and Cartridge
the new greys for 2018.

arjowiggins

Conqueror

ESTD 1888

MADE IN
SCOTLAND

Arjowiggins Creative Papers are distributed by Antalis
arjowigginscreativepapers.com/conqueror

KINFOLK

FOUNDER & CREATIVE DIRECTOR
Nathan Williams

EDITOR-IN-CHIEF
Julie Cirelli

EDITOR
John Clifford Burns

DEPUTY EDITOR
Harriet Fitch Little

ART DIRECTOR
Christian Møller Andersen

DESIGN DIRECTOR
Alex Hunting

BRAND DIRECTOR
Amy Woodroffe

COPY EDITOR
Rachel Holzman

CEO
Peter Hildebrandt

COMMUNICATIONS DIRECTOR
Jessica Gray

PRODUCER
Cecilie Jegsen

CASTING DIRECTOR
Sarah Bunter

SALES & DISTRIBUTION DIRECTOR
Frédéric Mähl

ADVERTISING DIRECTOR
Pamela Mullinger

BUSINESS OPERATIONS MANAGER
Kasper Schademan

STUDIO MANAGER
Aryana Tajdivand-Echevarria

EDITORIAL ASSISTANTS
Lena Hunter
Garett Nelson

SALES ASSISTANT
Zuzanna Gesla

CONTRIBUTING EDITORS
Michael Anastassiades
Jonas Bjerre-Poulsen
Andrea Codrington Lippke
Ilse Crawford
Margot Henderson
Leonard Koren
Hans Ulrich Obrist
Amy Sall
Matt Willey

STYLING, HAIR & MAKEUP
Kimberly Ade
Carola Bianchi
Line Bille
Maria Blaisse
Victoria Bond
Sébastien Cambos
Hirokazu Endo
Debbie Hsieh
Giovanni Iovine
Shukeel Murtaza
Kenneth Pihl Nissen
David Nolan
Maria Olsson
Kingsley Tao
Christos Vourlis
Amber Watkins
Phebe Wu

PUBLICATION DESIGN
Alex Hunting

CROSSWORD
Molly Young

WORDS
Alex Anderson
Ellie Violet Bramley
Katie Calautti
Mansi Choksi
Carole Corm
Djassi DaCosta Johnson
Harriet Fitch Little
Chris Frey
Alia Gilbert
Pamela K. Johnson
MacKenzie Lewis Kassab
Molly Mandell
Sala Elise Patterson
Debika Ray
Asher Ross
Tristan Rutherford
Laura Rysman
Charles Shafaieh
Pip Usher

PHOTOGRAPHY
Anna Beeke
Simone Cavadini
Pelle Crépin
Chalkie Davies
Iringó Demeter
Christopher Ferguson
Emma Hartvig
Todd Hido
T. Harrison Hillman
Ariel Huber
Hördur Ingason
Eric Lafforgue
Annie Lai
Fanny Latour-Lambert
Jae-An Lee
Danilo Scarpati
Jeanloup Sieff
Ryan Thompson
Marsý Hild Þórsdóttir
Zoltan Tombor
Dorte Tuladhar
David Uzochukwu
Samuel Zeller

info@kinfolk.com
www.kinfolk.com

Published by Ouur Media
Amagertorv 14, Level 1
1160 Copenhagen, Denmark

The views expressed in Kinfolk magazine are those of the respective contributors and are not necessarily shared by the company or its staff.

SUBSCRIBE
Kinfolk is published four times a year. To subscribe, visit kinfolk.com/subscribe or email us at info@kinfolk.com

CONTACT US
If you have questions or comments, please write to us at info@kinfolk.com. For advertising inquiries, get in touch at advertising@kinfolk.com

Printed in Canada by
Hemlock Printers Ltd.

danish design by · made by

LINDBERG

marset

Taking care of light

Welcome

Hair is dead matter—something to shampoo, shape and sigh over when it falls wrong (or falls out). However, it is also a powerfully important matter; a site of self-expression and a repository of cultural identity. Throughout history, hair has been used as shorthand to signal power and social affiliation. It continues to play crucial—and contested—roles in religion, industry, the arts and politics. "If I want to knock a story off the front page, I just change my hairstyle," Hillary Clinton once joked. Whether rebellious, ravishing or even quite unremarkable, hair reveals.

This issue of *Kinfolk* untangles the meaning of hair. In Toronto, we meet Jagmeet Singh, the leader of Canada's New Democratic Party, and his brother Gurratan. Unlike the incumbent US President (whose hair is as ridiculous as his politics), the Singhs are campaigning for "love and courage"—a message embodied in their personal observance of *kes*, the Sikh practice of leaving hair unshorn. "The whole point of kes in Sikhism is an acceptance of our natural way of being, accepting yourself in a deeper way," Jagmeet explains. "There's this incredibly strong social aspect to [hair]," adds Gurratan. "We can't hide who we are or where we're from."

Hair is also the catalyst for a conversation with Sherin Khankan, a Danish imam working not only to challenge Islamophobic dialogue but to redress patriarchal interpretations of Islam from her women-only mosque in Copenhagen. Elsewhere, writer Pamela K. Johnson combs through a history of Diana Ross' ever-changing hair; author Carole Corm recounts how one hairdresser found his Beirut salon caught in the crossfire of Lebanon's civil war; and we look at what happens when hair turns up in the wrong places—as far afield as food and forensic science.

Also in this issue, we meet Helen Nonini, a Milanese brand strategist who offers us her hard-earned wisdom in the art of professional problem solving. The trick? Decoding the human heart. Harriet Fitch Little pursues the same strategy as she traces the evolution of matchmaking—from the *shtetls* of yore to the smartphones of today. In Mumbai, we visit an architectural practice harnessing the city's chaotic energy to create sanctuary-like interiors, and are inspired to find our own pockets of urban enjoyment in generic hotel rooms, late night strolls, and even the relentless pestering of the humble housefly.

JOHN CLIFFORD BURNS

"In a Willy Wonka world, you don't try to grasp at logic."
HELEN NONINI — P.42

CONTENTS

Photograph: Danilo Scarpati

kvadrat

PART THREE

Hair

"We can't be passive when we see injustice happening around us."
JAGMEET SINGH — P.136

PART FOUR

Directory

Photograph: Emma Hartvig

Arctander Chair
Designed in 1944 by Philip Arctander
Relaunched in 2016 by Paustian

paustian

Aēsop.

Aesop was established in Melbourne in 1987. Our objective has always been to formulate skin, hair, and body care products of the finest quality. Given our longstanding engagement with the arts, it is a pleasure to partner with *Kinfolk* magazine to support the Kinfolk Gallery in Copenhagen.

To discover more about our offerings, you are invited to visit Aesop stores and counters globally, and to browse online at **aesop.com**

'Arrange whatever pieces come your way.' **Virginia Woolf**

18 — 40

Starters

ALEX ANDERSON

A History of Regret

The case against what ifs and if onlys.

In a deep black pit lies a prone figure menaced by an enraged and partially disemboweled bison. Head back, eyes wide, arms and fingers outspread, the man in the cave at Lascaux, France, confronts the knowledge of death. This drawing, the world's oldest narrative depiction of a human being, may convey one man's mortal surprise and sorrow, but it also seems to say something momentous about humanity. French philosopher Georges Bataille proposed that it reveals the instant, some 17,000 years ago, when we separated from the animal world. He links the birth of art with the birth of human history. But if this picture recounts the beginning of history, it also tells of the beginning of regret. "If only I had thrown my spear a little straighter…," the hunter might have been lamenting. Beyond this momentary thought, in the imminence of death, he seems to gaze into his unspooling past—wishing, perhaps, that life had been different.

The etymology of "regret" connects it to an old French term for bewailing the dead. Regret belongs with grief, but signifies more than mourning. To use the words of Confucian scholar Michael Ing, "Regret means a kind of sorrowful longing for things to be otherwise." Confucius considered regret, however painful, to be a proper feeling, because it arises from moral reflection on personal actions or from thoughts about how unavoidable conditions in the world can harm things we value. It can certainly lead to improvement: Thinking "I wish I had done things differently," or, "I wish things were not the way they are," might be the catalyst for positive action.

At about the same time, give or take 100 years, Plato was also reflecting on regret and how to avoid it. His account of Socrates preparing for death by execution is that of a man unwilling to pass out of this world with personal regrets—although he certainly wished his circumstances could have been different. His friends, Plato among them, pleaded with Socrates to find some means of escape, but Socrates rebuffed them, saying he would neither dissimulate nor grovel to survive. "The difficulty, my friends," he said, "is not to avoid death, but to avoid unrighteousness." His admonition in Plato's *Apology* that "The unexamined life is not worth living," has served as an almost eternal guide for avoiding personal regret.

This statement could be understood as the theme for one of the best-known tales of regret in English: that of Ebenezer Scrooge, the "squeezing, wrenching, grasping, scraping, clutching, covetous, old sinner" in Charles Dickens' early Victorian story, *A Christmas Carol*. It depicts a smugly unexamined life jolted into righteousness. Scrooge's long-dead business partner appears as a ghost and bemoans his own unalterable lifetime of greed. He offers Scrooge a way out of the sad fate he suffers—the most painful aspect of which is the fact that in death "no space of regret can make amends for one life's opportunity misused." Aided by three spiritual guides, Scrooge reemerges after a long night of moral reflection determined to seek life's opportunities for virtue and generosity: "He knew what path lay straight before him, and he took it."

Regret, in our own time, can act as a powerful frame for action—as long as we avoid it. The rallying cry of "No regrets!" for sports teams and graduating classes is persuasive. It's also more uplifting than Friedrich Nietzsche's 19th-century "formula for human greatness": the concept of *amor fati*, meaning an enthusiastic acceptance of one's fate.

Sadly, for many people, this defiance comes too late to be helpful. Specialists on dying and end-of-life care note how frequently regret clings to death. Accordingly, they provide helpful, instructive lists of reflective measures to follow in life: Be kind; take things less seriously; work less; take risks. The advice to take risks underlies the 21st century's newest tool for regret avoidance, the "bucket list"—an ambitious personal catalog of things to do before dying. One thing that should perhaps be on everyone's list: a visit to the Shaft of the Dead Man at Lascaux.

In a world where winning is what matters, regret—the emotional aftershock of failure—is too often treated as a pathological emotion.

Photograph: Iringó Demeter

Bad Rocks

From nature, take nothing but memories. Or be sorry.

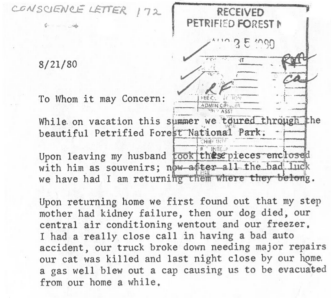

In Arizona's Petrified Forest National Park, the fossilized trees look like rocks filled with minerals including quartz, amethyst and cobalt. They are dazzling—so dazzling, in fact, that visitors frequently pocket pieces despite all the signs prohibiting them from doing so. I did it myself, taking two tiny pieces of rock when I stopped at the park on a road trip a few years back. But many people who remove the rocks end up wishing desperately that they hadn't, often returning them in the mail. "They are beautiful, but I can't enjoy them," scrawl capital letters on one note. "Take these miserable rocks and put them back into the rainbow forest, for they have caused pure havoc in my love life and Cheryl's too," pleads another letter written on torn-out notebook paper and signed "Dateless + Desperate."

These "conscience letters" are a few of the thousands received by the park, and compiled in the book *Bad Luck, Hot Rocks* by artists Ryan Thompson and Phil Orr. Thompson says that many of the culprits return their pocketed treasures to the park with stories of trials and tribulations: "They span this entire range of human experience,

from absolutely tragic—people dying at or near the park, people getting cancer—to things that are commonplace or even silly."

The origins of such superstitions are hazy. Many psychologists think that finding reason for adversity gives us greater feelings of control over our lives. Thompson notes that phenomena like these often occur in places that had or have a strong Native American presence. "Perhaps people are wrestling with or trying to understand their relationship to the land," he says.

The catch is that the wood can never actually be returned, because rangers are unable to verify its exact origins. Instead, it is placed atop the park's "conscience pile" on a private service road.

Recently, I found myself making the same trip before moving abroad. Once again I stopped at the Petrified Forest, this time to return the stolen property. Moving halfway across the world was going to be difficult enough, and I didn't want any bad luck coming with me. Perhaps the petrified wood had nothing to do with my bad luck, but it felt good to have it off my hands and closer to where it belonged.

GONGSHI
by Molly Mandell

Collections of various kinds have served as creative inspiration for their owners: Writer Vladimir Nabokov had a passion for butterflies and artist Andy Warhol was a collector of cookie jars. In China, however, there has long been another item admired by painters and poets: Rocks. These are not just any rocks but *gongshi*, or scholar's stones, which have been shaped by erosion. As early as the Tang dynasty, a set of criteria existed to evaluate such stones: thinness (*shou*), openness (*tou*), wrinkling (*zhou*) and perforation (*lou*). In *Spirit Stones: The Ancient Art of the Scholar's Rock*, gongshi expert Kemin Hu argues that these rocks do more than stimulate creativity, they "share a telepathic connection with human souls." (Top: Large basalt abstract sculpture. Center: Extra-large lapis box. Bottom: Ceramic handmade Cubist sculpture. (All objects are Collected by The Line.)

Letter: Courtesy of Ryan Thompson. Right Photographs: Courtesy of Collected by The Line.

A short guide to making eye contact.

Photograph: Fanny Latour-Lambert

CHARLES SHAFAIEH

Just Looking

Eye contact, to many, signals interest and trust. Doctors are taught to look patients in the eye, job interviewers favor those who meet their gaze, and even babies prefer direct, rather than oblique, stares. That our pupils dilate when we find someone attractive—a change that is mirrored if the feeling is mutual—is something we've known for a long time. In Renaissance Italy, women would go to the lengths of inducing dilation with belladonna extract, unaware it could cause blindness.

Serbian performance artist Marina Abramović considers eye contact a powerful mode of communication. In 2010, at New York's Museum of Modern Art, Abramović spent 700 hours sitting in silence as nearly 1,400 people sat across from her and met her gaze. "There's nothing happening. There's no plot, no crescendo… There's no beginning or end," she said in a 2017 interview. "There's just you and me. It's about eyes and gaze. This is true communication…"

Challenging as this intimate experience may seem (more than 3.3 seconds of eye contact makes many uncomfortable), our eyes may be evolutionarily inclined toward it. Our sclera—the white surrounding the iris—is much larger than in other primates, possibly so that we might see in which direction others are looking. Regardless of what our cultural norms dictate about locking eyes, we cannot help but notice the direction of someone's gaze.

And yet, the assumption that peering into someone's eyes causes heightened understanding may need reexamining. According to a 2016 Japanese study, researchers discovered that making eye contact activates the same parts of the brain used to complete various complex mental tasks. We look away, they concluded, due to overstimulation; without doing so, we may not have enough capacity for deep thinking.

When given a cognitively taxing task—like solving a mathematical problem—which forces you to delve into your mind, averting your gaze may be the better tactic. But when you are required to commune with someone—to empathize with them or take them into your confidence—then nothing else, no words or other bodily gestures, can suffice quite like locking eyes.

Photography by Helene Binet

MICHAELANASTASSIADES

www.michaelanastassiades.com

In Seoul, a designer emerges with a subdued style for strong women.

PIP USHER

Shinhye Suk

Photograph: Jae-An Lee

Shinhye Suk creates clothes for powerful women. After studying at Parsons School of Design and cutting her teeth at designer Derek Lam's headquarters in New York, Suk returned to her native South Korea in 2016. She was attracted by Seoul's legendary fabric market, vibrant manufacturing industry and affordable rent. Eighteen months and two collections later, her label, Lehho, has established itself as an elegant alternative to the city's dominant street-style aesthetic.

Lehho is a relatively young label. What's the vision behind it? Lehho seems simple, but if you look at the garments you can tell that each piece was created with complexity. Thought-out details and attention to the character of the fabric are critical.

Tell me about the women you have in mind. I am drawn to strong, independent women. For the spring/summer 2018 collection, I was struck by Tilda Swinton in *A Bigger Splash*. I was fascinated by how she dressed in the movie, and how she fits in so beautifully to the setting.

What childhood memories do you have of fashion? My mom really paid attention to how my siblings and I were dressed. I remember when it was class president election day and I was one of the candidates. She styled my hair in two braids and dressed me in a beautiful white blouse paired with a black pleated skirt, black stockings, shiny black patent Mary Jane shoes and a decorative red cardigan. And guess what? I became a class leader. I'm sure her professional styling helped—and maybe that's how I ended up obsessed with the "polished" look.

What's the idea behind your latest collection? It's a playful examination of how clothing has traditionally been a social marker—the serving class is meant to have little identity, while carefully crafted pieces in indulgent fabrics were reserved for the waited-upon. I was inspired by Octave Mirbeau's novel, *The Diary of a Chambermaid*, which examines masters, servants and morality in the 19th century.

As an entrepreneur, what are the biggest challenges that you face? I'm involved in every single part of the business, but this is also one of the most rewarding aspects of being my own boss. I've learned so much more than if I'd worked for someone else. Now, I even know how to make a mini envelope for extra buttons.

How do you unwind? I play this game on my phone where I make ice cream and serve customers in an ice cream shop. It sounds silly, but it really helps take my mind off work before bed.

David Uzochukwu

A prolific photographer comes of age.

Artwork: David Uzochukwu. Courtesy of Galerie Number 8.

Nothing is ever quite as it seems in David Uzochukwu's photography. His subjects—often Uzochukwu himself—are captured balled up in never-ending bed linen, floating on rivers made of clouds or melting into lush landscapes. Through elaborate production and post-production, the 19-year-old creates hypnotic images that ache with strange emotion: The faces he photographs appear wrought by unnamed pains and joys.

A self-taught photographer, Uzochukwu began shooting at age 10, when he discovered his mother's point-and-shoot camera. He took photos (and posted online) relentlessly until he got his break a few years later when he did his first editorial shoot at the age of 14. Now based in Vienna, Uzochukwu continues to shoot while working toward a degree in philosophy. The setting feels right for someone whose photographs are born of emotion, executed with academic rigor and crafted with a philosopher's penchant for deep reflection.

You often photograph your subjects in seemingly boundless natural landscapes. What's the appeal of the infinite? In real life, I'm drawn to environments that aren't obviously man-made and that have not obviously been influenced by man. I find nature very calming and inspiring in all of its beauty and cruelty, and in its existence, which is completely independent of people. Visually it's appealing because of the vast amount of color, and the textures that keep repeating themselves.

Your favorite subject to shoot seems to be yourself. Why? It's more practical to shoot myself because I'm always available! That's one part of it. And then there's the fact that portraiture is incredibly intimate. It's partly to do with not having to communicate a vision but knowing exactly where I want things to go. [Self-portraiture] feels like it's truly and entirely a product of my own. To know that no one else is involved in the creation of the piece is fantastic—very cathartic.

Which growing pains have you worked through in your photography? Anything weighing on my mind can be worked through like that—frustration, boredom, longing, a deep existential crisis now and then. Being a teenager, a brother, a son, a friend, a minority, a human—it's never-ending material for issues. I always know when I need to lose some emotional baggage, but I don't necessarily vivisect the emotion before it's locked in place visually.

You're represented by Galerie Number 8, which represents artists that explore cultural identity. How does your work do that? My work is such an intimate reflection of who I am. My mother is from Austria and my father is from Nigeria. I was born and raised in Austria, as well as in Luxembourg and Belgium. It was a lot of going back and forth, a lot of belonging and not belonging, and always somehow being a minority and being excluded in a way. There's this yearning for home and at the same time, there's a sense of home everywhere.

With all the different geographies running through your life story, which places in the world inspire you? When I was in Oregon a couple of years ago it felt like someone had put visuals of my dreams out there into reality. It was a very surreal feeling. But regularly I'm surprised by how incredibly beautiful landscapes are right in my backyard. Any place with a wide-open sky has a very high chance of touching me.

Where do you want to take your work in your 20s? I've always tried to chase that one image; I'm very single-image focused right now. But I'm trying to expand and make larger bodies of work. Also, I'd like to do more motion film, and see how I can incorporate that into my process.

People make a lot of the fact that you've achieved so much at such a young age. Does that feel like pressure or is it freeing? It's definitely freeing. I'm excited about where I am right now, with opportunities that are absolutely insane to think about. I just consider myself very fortunate to have found something that I truly enjoy and that I can see myself doing for a very long time.

"It's more practical to shoot myself because I'm always available."

Uzochukwu's *Giving Way* is a 2016 series inspired by Chinua Achebe, whose novels documented the fracturing of society in colonial Nigeria.

DJASSI DACOSTA JOHNSON

Brendan Fernandes

An interview about rigid discipline and supple bodies.

Brendan Fernandes is a multimedia artist with the mind—and the body—of a dancer. Not surprisingly, he studied ballet as a teenager and modern dance in college before settling on a career as a visual artist. A Kenyan-Indian-Canadian, his 2008 video *Foe* saw him trying to speak the accents of his various ancestral languages and was exhibited at New York's Guggenheim Museum. His latest piece, *The Master and Form*, is part homage to, part damning critique of, the classical ballet world of his childhood. The installation and performance series, presented in collaboration with the designer Norman Kelley at the Graham Foundation in Chicago, explores "themes of mastery and discipline within the culture of ballet." Performers dance around scaffolding intended to help them push their bodies to new limits, whereas Fernandes, now 38, assumes the symbolically loaded position of the highly disciplinary ballet master.

You were a ballet dancer as a teenager. Why didn't you stick with it? I started doing community ballet at 12 years old and eventually started taking classes with the national ballet. But I was never actually enrolled in the school; my family didn't have the resources. In those classes I was already feeling scrutinized: My feet were too flat,

they criticized my neck, etcetera. But I was really flexible and had long legs so they were like, "You should go to modern [dance]." I studied modern in college, but I was always doing visual arts. I remember thinking to myself, "How will I do both of these?"

In the end, you embarked on a career as a visual artist. How did you find your way back to dance? In 2009, I did my first piece working with dancers. It was called *Encomium* and I was looking at the queer body and thinking about the idea of brokenness. It's based on Plato's *Symposium* where Phaedrus says that love is asymmetrical: You'll never fully fulfill love, it will always break apart. I talked about that as a metaphor for love but also for this breaking of the body, as it falls out of this love relationship with dance.

Your latest piece focused on the power dynamics within ballet, and the rigidity of the form. Where did that interest come from? There's a history in visual arts that teaches critical thinking: People are making political commentary, writing about the world. With dancers, we're not allowed to be critical. For me, there's a power dynamic that's not talked about within ballet—I mean, we call our teachers "master."

You seem drawn to the image of the ballet master as an emblem of control. I learned my dedication and discipline as an artist and person through dance. You have these things that put you in perfect positions that are almost torturous—reminiscent of devices that were used in colonial inquisitions—but they're also, you know, somewhat kinky because there's the sense of pleasure and pain. I remember dancing once, and I had dropped something on my toe beforehand—I definitely had broken it and the toenail had fallen off. I just taped it and went and danced the whole performance. It felt amazing. The resilience and threshold of pain that a dancer has is phenomenal.

Why cast a critical eye on an art form which you also obviously revere? Critical yes, but I'm searching for ways of newness within that. That's why I call these art spaces "queer" because there are many possibilities. I didn't become a ballet dancer, but ballet has opened my artistic perspective. It's part of my culture and as artists we represent our culture through our work. I'm fifth-generation Kenyan-born, but Indian with a Portuguese last name. That's my identity, but there is ballet, punk, rock music... those subcultures formed who I am.

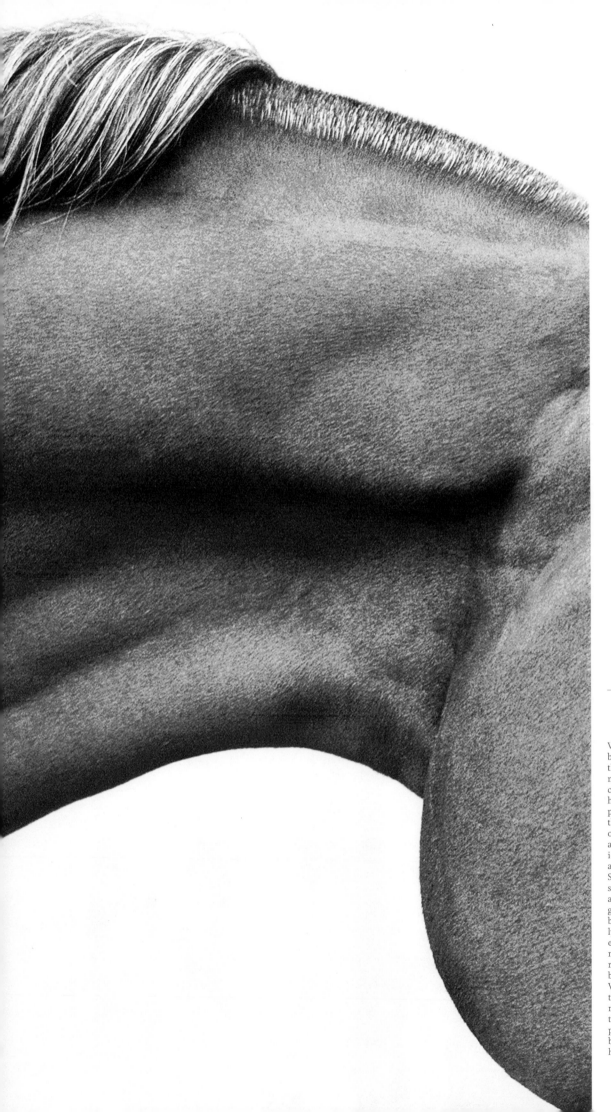

MUSCLE MEMORY

by Harriet Fitch Little

When Admiral Nelson lost his arm in battle in 1797, he gained a new faith in the afterlife: The admiral could feel the muscles in his missing limb move so convincingly that he was certain his arm had become a ghost. Two centuries later, phantom limb syndrome remains one of the most mysterious medical conditions on record. Experienced by the majority of amputees, the sensations it brings are vivid and precise: a too-tight wedding ring, a dribble of scalding water, a stiff joint. Somehow—and there is still no consensus as to exactly how—amputation causes a rewiring of nerve pathways to the brain, generating feelings where there should be none. For many people, these ghostly appendages are physically painful and emotionally upsetting—a constant reminder of traumas best forgotten. But on rare occasions, they have the potential to be life-enhancing. Austrian pianist Paul Wittgenstein, who lost his right arm in the First World War, continued to commission music for both hands. According to one former pupil, Wittgenstein told his protégés to "Trust his choice of fingering because he felt every finger of his right hand." *Photography by Dorte Tuladhar.*

ALEX ANDERSON

Bird Grammar

Learning the strict, squawky syntax of birdsong.

Few sounds are more pleasant than the chorus of birds on a spring morning. Robins start in before the sun rises; their clear, bubbling songs echo across the darkened rooftops. Soon, song sparrows jump up on bushes to join them, and other voices from deeper hiding places. Raucous calls of jays and crows punctuate the melodies. Woodpeckers, lacking strong vocal talents, pound out rhythms on lampposts and house sidings. Whether in Cairo or Copenhagen, a similar chorus formed of local accents rises with the warming sun. Peaceful, isn't it?

Not really. What we actually hear when stepping into the fragrant air is aggressive or lascivious shouting. As behavioral biologists Sanne Moorman and Johan J. Bolhuis have written: "The main function of song seems to be defense of territory and mate attraction." In other words, each warble, trill and twitter in that mainly male chorale is either yelling "Stay back!" or "Come hither!" And these are no ordinary shouts. Ornithologists have shown that songbirds triple their daily energy expenditure to convey these messages. The birds are bellowing.

There is subtlety, though, because males must distinguish themselves and demonstrate their fitness for parental duties. Each bird's song therefore differs slightly from another's in tone, speed, inflection, accent and even vocabulary. Birds also vary their message according to context. When their young are hatching, for example, the "Stay back" holler wins out. These messages consist of multiple syllables joined into phrases, assembled as songs, and delivered in clusters. Typically, a bird repeats the same song cluster over and over with minor variations throughout the day and season. Some sing only a few syllables, while others offer up songs of astounding complexity.

The Pacific wren, a tiny brown sprite that lurks in the forests of the Pacific Northwest, sings perhaps North America's most complicated birdsong. In a remarkable study, biologist Beatrice Van Horne found that an individual wren might use 10 or 11 different types of syllables (think of these as its alphabet) combined according to distinct rules into as many as 327 different songs. This means that their songs appear to observe rules of syntax. That is, their patterns of syllables carry specific meanings, much like properly constructed sentences do. More recent studies of California thrashers and Bengalese finches reinforce this conclusion: Birds mean what they sing.

Possibly the most remarkable realization these careful studies provoke is that birdsong and human speech follow similar phonetic sequences. Birdsong may sound sweet to the ear because birds prefer the kinds of patterns and rhythms we prefer. Birds and humans share, it seems, a basic "universal grammar." Even so, it's worth remembering that the robin singing from a treetop is not your friend; he's bellowing "Stay back!"

Just like humans, birds have regional accents. In the San Francisco Bay Area alone, the white-crowned sparrow sings in more than 10 different dialects.

The Suite Spot

On the public privacy and fleeting intimacy of hotel rooms.

Hotels thrust their occupants into a state of limbo even as they serve as a bulwark from the outside world. They can be both a welcome refuge and unsettlingly cold; homelike in their decor but cell-like in that what is there is often nailed down, and certainly not yours to keep. If part of a large chain, the rooms appear similar regardless of location, as Swiss photographer Roger Eberhard reveals in his photographic study *Standard* which showcases the unnerving sameness of Hilton hotel rooms around the world.

That there are no personal connections to the objects in a hotel room can, however, prove stimulating, particularly for artists. Maya Angelou wrote in near-barren hotel rooms when on the road—but also in her hometown. In the same way that Samuel Beckett flourished when he switched from writing in English to French—a language in which *mère* was just a word, emptied of all sentimental, maternal resonances—this emotionless environment allowed Angelou to continue writing. "I go into the room and I feel as if all my beliefs are suspended," she said, in *The Paris Review.* "No milkmaids, no flowers, nothing. I just want to *feel* and then when I start to work I'll remember." Cleaned every morning and returned to their original state, these rooms defy their inhabitants' urge to leave their marks and yet invite them to keep trying, night after night.

The imagination can be invigorated within these rooms too, as snippets of conversation or mere voices, the words too hazy to discern, can be heard from neighboring rooms. Sometimes even a door is shared between strangers—a portal imbued with mysterious potential. What is happening behind that door, in that room that looks just like your own? Each guest is just one in an infinite series resting their heads on that pillow each night, dreaming there just as countless others have before them.

It is no accident that Alain Resnais and Alain Robbe-Grillet set their enigmatic 1961 film, *Last Year at Marienbad*, in a baroque hotel. Its nameless characters traverse seemingly endless corridors that repeat themselves like Escher's stairs. The movie set—a concatenation of multiple filming locations fused together through tricks of editing—reinforces the disorienting nature that so many hotels share. You might emerge from an elevator and move mechanically toward your room only to realize, upon trying your key, that you are on the wrong floor altogether.

In Paul Auster's novel *The Brooklyn Follies*, a character details his impression of hotels, which had fascinated him as a child despite never staying in one. "The sole purpose of a hotel was to make you happy and comfortable, and once you signed the register and went upstairs to your room, all you had to do was ask for something and it was yours," he says. "A hotel represented the promise of a better world, a place that was more than just a place, but an opportunity, a chance to live inside your dreams."

As rewarding as that promise might seem, it has a melancholic underside. Though some may have their permanent address at the Plaza in New York City, hotels really exist for the itinerant. Guests may experience that utopic hope within the walls of these temporary homes, but that feeling must always remain there, for those who come later to enjoy—and leave behind in turn.

Diane von Furstenberg once said: "When you get into a hotel room, you lock the door, and you know there is a secrecy, there is a luxury, there is fantasy."

In *The Sorrows of Young Werther*, Goethe notes that actions we judge as malicious are more likely the result of "misunderstandings and neglect."

DEBIKA RAY

On Judging Others

How to find the benefit of doubt.

Figures at the center of a public scandal often find themselves facing the "stupid or evil?" conundrum. A chief executive whose company has dodged paying tax and a celebrity recorded using offensive language might find themselves facing the same choice: Claim ignorance/incompetence (stupid) or admit full responsibility for the nefarious act (evil). Society is generally more forgiving of stupidity than deliberate malice, so most people opt for the former strategy.

But is it always a bluff? Consider Hanlon's Razor, an aphorism that is generally stated as: "Never attribute to malice that which is adequately explained by stupidity." Its origins are hazy but its meaning clear: Don't jump to the conclusion that someone's actions are guided by bad intentions.

Hanlon's Razor is a wise principle that too often goes ignored. On social media, you frequently witness small missteps resulting in fierce and arguably misplaced wrath. In 2012, for example, a healthcare worker's life was turned upsidedown after a friend posted a photo of her at Arlington National Cemetery on Facebook. She was flipping the bird and pretending to shout in front of a sign that said "silence and respect"—part of a running joke between the two friends of taking contrarian photos (smoking in front of a "no smoking" sign, for example). You may think it stupid, but was it an act of intentional malevolence deserving of mass public shaming, death threat and sacking?

The enlargement and anonymization of the public realm by the internet seem to have exacerbated our tendency to assume the worst in others, while blurring the boundaries of acceptable behavior. Screeching condemnation of a sort that would be unthinkable in person is largely acceptable online.

When considering how to judge and react to someone's behavior in this context, Florida-based etiquette coach Patricia Rossi suggests putting yourself in the offender's shoes. "None of us are perfect, and we do misstep—if we were being videotaped 24/7, how much of what you say do you think would be jumbled up or [badly] phrased?" she asks, advising against publicly calling out offensive behavior. "Do it in private—or you'll only cause the other person to be defensive."

The moral demands of Hanlon's Razor may occasionally be hard to stomach. It compels you to consider the ravings of others first as stupid, not monstrous. But it also means you'll be less vulnerable to conspiracy theories that arise from the assumption that people are always up to no good. Perhaps you'll also, in a small way, contribute to the creation of a kinder public discourse.

ELLIE VIOLET BRAMLEY

Word: Yugen

The mysteries of the universe, distilled into one word.

Etymology: Made up of two Japanese characters. The first, "yu," means dim or difficult to see. The second, "gen," originally described the dark, tranquil color of the universe—something calm and deep.

Meaning: The meaning depends on the context; the explanation most commonly offered is an awareness of the universe that triggers an emotional response too deep and mysterious for words. You may find that definition opaque, but it is an attempt to explain in words something that is fundamentally ineffable. Or you may feel a spark of recognition somewhere deep within. This is likely a feeling you've experienced but never before had a word for.

To best wrap your head around a word that words fail, it's better to contemplate less its literal meaning and more the situations that might inspire it. Looking to the cosmos, for example, can resonate in a profound way. Perhaps you've experienced *yugen* when you've gazed at stars, and really seen them, with a clarity that only comes from being away from the city and its halo of light pollution. And maybe the feeling deepened when you realized that the light you're seeing is years old and has traveled across trillions of miles to reach you.

"Wandering along through pine trees beside a stream," is how 20th-century British philosopher Alan Watts begins his own musing on the quality of yugen. Best known for popularizing eastern philosophy for western audiences, Watts continues: "Where is he going? Where is the stream going? Where are the clouds going? Where are the birds going? We don't really know. They are wandering on."

A fundamental concept in Japanese art and culture, this sense of unknowability and mystery is reflected in the description offered a few centuries earlier by playwright Zeami Motokiyo: "To watch the sun sink behind a flower clad hill… To contemplate the flight of wild geese seen and lost among the clouds."

Yugen, then, has to do not with a world that exists beyond our own, but with the depths of the world we live in. And if we can learn to flex our imaginations, it's a feeling that all of us can experience anytime, any place.

SPACE BUBBLES
by Harriet Fitch Little

On the International Space Station, bubbles don't burst like they do on earth. As there is no gravity to upset their delicate constitution, the soapy spheres can withstand being poked—painted, even—by curious astronauts. NASA scientist Don Pettit, who has completed two long stints on the ISS, spent his free time on board experimenting with surface tension. Among his achievements were a set of "Russian nesting" bubbles, created by injecting smaller bubbles into larger ones, and bubbles that sat on top of speakers and jigged along to popular tunes. For those of us back on earth and bound by gravity, blowing bubbles remains a short-lived pleasure. But the orbs' form is to be found replicated in many captivating—and far more durable—designs around the home, such as Frama's Atelier Globe 125 bulb (top), Oswald Haerdtl's Candy Dish III (center), or OYOY's glass paperweight (bottom).

Left Photograph: Samuel Zeller, Right Photographs: Courtesy of Frama and The Line

Is unfinished art a failure, or an opportunity?

A work of art may appear unfinished for an array of reasons, including frustration, disinterest, or the artist's death. The effect is often uncanny. In the case of a painting, subjects drawn only as outlines may seem to have vanished completely from the canvas; inversely, a blank background might make discernible figures float ghostlike in an empty, waiting-to-be-defined space. People might seem monstrous too, with a head drawn but not a face, or a body missing limbs.

These in *media res* creations have long inspired conjecture about artists' biographies and psyches—as if they let us see the hand in mid-motion, the artist in mid-thought, and witness the work as only the artist might, before it was deemed fit for public consumption and enjoyment. Many artists work with a rough sketch first —an under-drawing—which, when visible, can seem somewhat scandalous, like glimpsing someone unclothed.

Seeing an unfinished piece makes visible the unfinishable quality of all art. "A poem is never finished. It is only abandoned," W. H. Auden once commented, paraphrasing Paul Valéry and alluding to society's misguided fetishizing of finished products. As the American artist Robert Morris argues in a 1969 essay, "The notion that a work is an irreversible process ending in a status icon-object no longer has much relevance." James Joyce's *Finnegans Wake* had demonstrated this decades earlier, its first and last lines connecting like a Mobius strip and perpetually delaying "the end." Like folktales passed by word of mouth across generations, the stories we repeat to friends and family are unfinished too, changing, even just slightly, with each telling. Finishing remains a dangerous notion, for the risk of over-finishing is perpetual. Like the near-blind buffalo hunted by Native Americans—who would trick the animals by causing a stampede that would lead them, unwittingly, over a cliff's edge—the artist crosses the line between under- and overwrought in an instant, without realizing it until experiencing a sinking plunge. But they might take comfort in the fact that even those belabored and overworked pieces are not truly "finished"—at least not in terms of the relationship between the piece and the spectator. As Belgian artist Luc Tuymans argues, "Every work has a weak point, a breaking point, which is where you enter the image." Art then must not be considered static. Rather, like any human, it never is but is always *becoming*.

CHARLES SHAFAIEH

Half the Picture

MACKENZIE LEWIS KASSAB

Lauren Ridloff

A former Miss Deaf America settles in on Broadway.

Photograph: Zoltan Tombor, Styling: Debbie Hsieh

Lauren Ridloff does nothing half-way. One of the actress's earliest screen appearances was in *Love Me Now*, John Legend's poignant music video that has amassed over 15 million views. She appeared shortly after in the Palme d'Or-nominated film *Wonderstruck*, directed by Todd Haynes and starring Julianne Moore and Michelle Williams. It's only fitting, then, that Ridloff's first professional stage gig should be a leading role on Broadway. The Brooklyn-based former Miss Deaf America recently made her theater debut in Mark Medoff's award-winning play *Children of a Lesser God*, directed by Kenny Leon. She plays Sarah Norman, a deaf woman who falls in love with a hearing man.

How would you describe your relationship to the role of Sarah in *Children of a Lesser God*? Finding Sarah was something I had to work hard at. In the beginning, I saw Sarah as a vitriolic woman who was furious at the world, and I wanted to protect her. I wanted to make her likable, relatable. Somewhere during the process, I fell in love with Sarah and her glorious flaws. That was when I was able to let her shine.

Sarah and I are obviously deaf, so it's a given that we experienced similar forms of lowered expectations, intrusive benevolence and acts of ignorance. What ties us together on a much deeper level is that we both kept the same resolve to not use our voices. It was a con-scious decision that I made at age 13, when I decided I found no use for my voice and told my family that I was going to turn it off. And I did until last summer. That experience was cathartic for both of us.

Did you have any childhood heroes? I grew up around people who were different from me in terms of how they perceived the world. It wasn't until high school that I met more people who mirrored me—people who grew up signing, relying on all other senses except for hearing. In terms of female empowerment, one of my earliest heroes was Frida Kahlo. My mother was studying art in school at the time, and she had Kahlo's books lying around the house. I fell in love with the artist's self-portraits. She was fearless in how she depicted herself to the world. Her back injury was the impetus of her art career. I relate to how her physical limitation became a vehicle of freedom. She used art to connect and communicate with the world on an intimately personal level.

You taught Kenny Leon sign language as he prepared to direct *Children of a Lesser God*. What was he like as a student? Kenny was always punctual and asked brilliant and very specific questions about Deaf culture. He was intrigued by the dynamics of the Deaf community today and how the play contributed to dialogues going on in present society. He was fearless in exploration—attributes he also shows as a director.

How did you feel when he eventually offered you the role? Kenny emailed me to tell me that the show's casting director, Bernie Telsey, wanted to pick my brain on deaf talent in New York City. I'm so glad I met Telsey unaware that he was going to ask me to do the reading. I didn't even know exactly what a reading meant. I just had a vague idea that it was the literal reading of a script, a semi-performance. That worked in my favor because I was able to start unpacking *Children of a Lesser God* almost casually, without the pressure of a possible Broadway role looming.

Do you have any pre-show rituals or good luck charms? Essential oils! Minutes before the curtains go up, I put a drop of oil into my hands and rub them together. Then I cup my hands, inhale and exhale a few times. That clears the mind and resets my breathing.

How does it feel to perform live? This is my first professional stage role, and wow, talk about a steep learning curve. Each day I'm learning something I should've known the day before. At the reading last year, I got past the worst of my fears—using my voice again for the first time in 26 years. I have a train of thought that has always helped me on stage, a nicer version of "imagine everybody in their undies." I just think about how

"I decided I found no use for my voice and told my family that I was going to turn it off."

A former Manhattan elementary school teacher, Ridloff secured her first stage role without even knowing she was up for the part.

"When running, it is the little steps that make up miles and miles."

the people who sit in the house are also part of the story we're telling. I believe they're engaged and receptive to the play's big idea: Stop judging and start listening.

***Children of a Lesser God* debuted in 1980. In what ways does the story deviate from a contemporary experience?** The play shows its age in some areas, such as technology for the Deaf. Since the play premiered almost 40 years ago, we've been introduced to Face-Time, texting and emailing. My neighbor used Siri's speech-to-text to talk with me, and I'd type back to him. Another neighbor downloaded an app to learn American Sign Language to talk with my sons, who are also Deaf. Then again, that's essentially me saying Shakespeare's *Romeo and Juliet* is outdated. Although *Children of a Lesser God* takes place in the late '70s and early '80s, the story itself is timeless.

Do you have any hobbies? I love wool. There's something about winding squishy skeins into firm-er cakes, then knitting those cakes into hats, cardigans, socks, things that my family and I can really wear. One Christmas I knitted an article of clothing for every single person in my family. Knitting is a testament of stamina and patience—exactly what I need to face each day.

Do you have a motto or maxim that guides you through life? It's a Yiddish saying that my mother-in-law shared with me a few years ago: *A bissel a bissel macht a grace shissel.* A little a little makes a big bowl. I find it relevant in every aspect of my life: mentally, physically, spiritually. While knitting, it is the little knot that eventually makes a large cardigan for my husband. When running, it is the little steps that make up miles and miles. While preparing for *Children of a Lesser God*, it is the small moments that I focus on that make up the big picture. *A bissel a bissel macht a grace shissel.* That saying gives me the confidence that I will arrive at where I want to be, as long as I focus on making the small steps.

When asked in a recent interview what marked Ridloff out as a talented actress, director Kenny Leon responded, "You can her her hands speak."

42 — 112

Features

H L E E N

Photography by Danilo Scarpati

In Milan, learning how to problem solve with a professional. Words by Laura Rysman

Outside the hallowed La Scala opera hall, the sidewalks are jammed with fashionistas vamping between runway shows. In Milan, fashion week manifests itself on the streets. Inside a bustling café, among the more distinguished representatives of the dressed-up throng, there's a young man in a gold pillbox hat strung with shoulder-length gold beads and a woman in a Gucci fur coat and rainbow-colored Chullo hat. Most diners are staring keenly at a more magnetic presence, however: a woman in a simple oversized cardigan and a high turban, holding court at the far edge of the black marble bar.

Admired for her acumen as well as for her eccentric headwear, Helen Nonini first made a name for herself as a professional problem solver for the exceedingly affluent, answering anxious calls to locate everything from a yoga instructor for dogs to a misplaced diamond-encrusted G-string. Though she is not famous, she is very recognizable, especially since becoming one of the ambassadors of a recent ad campaign for Pomellato jewelry. Vaulting from her reputation as a guru of taste and a master of missions impossible, she now heads her own independent agency for brand strategy.

Today, Nonini has met two friends and collaborators for coffee before we're scheduled to spend the afternoon together. To her right is the photographer Brigitte Niedermair, a collaborator on Nonini's art fabric project for the Dedar textile brand, while to her left sits *Corriere della Sera*'s art director, Gianluigi Colin.

"Helen is a woman of immense talents and intelligence," Colin pronounces theatrically over the clanging of porcelain demitasses from behind the coffee counter. "I used to have a hard time understanding clearly what she does, but now I get it. One could say that she is an anthropologist of communication."

For years, Nonini was a top steward at the luxury concierge service Quintessentially, a position she jokingly describes as being a "social assistant to bored rich people." She built her reputation as a problem solver there, through her psychological study of human nature, her talent for emotional manipulation (in the service of keeping people happy),

Helen wears a jacket, skirt, silk stockings and boots by Fendi.

FEATURES

and her almost maniacal research into the tastes and preferences of not only the people she served, but also their assistants as well as hotel staff, restaurant personnel, and anyone else who could help her obtain what she needed to satisfy her clients.

"You have to play to the six-year-old in every adult," she says, as she clinks her espresso cup into its dish and hands each of her friends a foil-wrapped chocolate. Her voice is husky and fast-paced as she glides over thoughts. "What makes them feel pampered, cared for, spoiled? Someone who spends 300,000 euros in a shop isn't impressed by fancy gifts—they'd prefer to have the exact song they want to hear come on the stereo when they step into their Ferrari, without having to think about it." And the way to find out someone's favorite song, apparently, is to pander to their assistants—Nonini's source for priceless details. "It's always a question of ego. When you nourish the ego of others—and you're not too heavy-handed about it—people feel appreciated, so they'll help you."

She is an expert in the game of behavior, and that game often involved convincing clients that the real-world substitution she was actually able to find was no less valuable than the impossible thing they desired. Want to do aerobics with Madonna? That proved too tough even for Nonini's wiles. Instead, that client received stage-side box seats and an autographed album.

"In a Willy Wonka world, you don't try to grasp at logic," says Nonini. "You just look for solutions." She sits dancer-straight on her high stool, long-necked and almond-eyed, the crown of her red and black leaf print turban extending her silhouette. "If someone says they need a pair of pigeons in Venice, I don't ask why. I just ask what gender."

Her parsing of human desires is a sixth sense she developed in a childhood of enduring outsiderdom. Nonini was born in Egypt with what she describes as four ethnicities in her blood—Sunni Iranian and Egyptian Shiite from her mother's side, and Italian from the diverse regions of Friuli and the Valtellina on her father's side. She found herself in a new school and a new country every three months, moving for her father's construction projects until the family settled in the Valtellina when she was 12. "In Egypt, I'm not an Egyptian. In Italy, I'm not an Italian. In Iran, I'm not an Iranian," Nonini says, leaning an elbow among the accumulating coffee cups. "I'm always different, always peering out at things from an angle. It's obvious that it changes your perspective." One becomes, above all, an observer of humanity.

As a teen in her first summer job, Nonini was already taking advantage of her zealous monitoring of others to get ahead. Working at a roadside pizza shop for tips, she kept detailed notes on the families that made regular pit stops at the restaurant; like a spy, she recorded the make of their cars, their license plate numbers, and their typical pizza orders. When she recognized a familiar car pulling up in the parking lot, she would place their order before the family had even walked in the door—anticipating desires, seeking to please customers, studying and obsessively recording the behavior of others at an age when most of us are deliriously self-centered.

"Be a lawyer," Nonini's mother commanded her, "or be a lawyer." But Nonini preferred sociology, was financially cut off by her parents and ended up in a desperate search for a way to support herself. She stumbled upon a well-paid position in finance, where she honed the skills of charm: sending secretaries presents and making herself known to their bosses by harnessing a database of the personal information (favorite music, wife's favorite music, children's names, birthdays) she extracted from them.

"For all those men at Morgan Stanley and Goldman Sachs, I was irrelevant because I was young, I was a woman, and I was trying to sell services to them," Nonini says. But she created what was essentially an early version of what she would go on to do at Quintessentially—playing to the egos of wealthy and powerful clients, and becoming indispensable through her studied research. "Working as a waiter is the smartest training someone can do for marketing," she says. But her past includes even more diverse professions: a year in India after her finance phase working with a charity opening schools, and, after Quintessentially, authoring a semi-fictional novel about the life of a problem solver.

Niedermair and Colin having departed, Nonini and I slide off our bar stools and head to the two-seater Smart car she has for the day. "People see me as a socialite—as someone who spends a lot of time at parties and grooming myself in front of the mirror." She maneuvers our diminutive car into traffic. "It's true I have over a hundred turbans," she confides, "But otherwise I'm a minimalist."

"If someone says they need a pair of pigeons in Venice, I don't ask why. I just ask what gender."

Helen wears a dress by Kenzo, turban by Altalen and ring by Pomellato.

A plastic crocodile and chicken arancini (at 3:00 a.m.) are among the more unusual items Helen was asked to source during her time as a professional problem solver.

We both need to be at the Missoni runway show in an hour. But first, to pick up her headwear for the evening, there's a visit to Altalen, the artisan milliner boutique that has been custom-creating Nonini's turbans since she began sporting them in 2012. Though she resists the burden of image, she acknowledges the public power it exerts. "When my photograph comes out in magazines, it does two things: It tells people who've lost their hair that wearing a turban can be considered cool, but it also reassures the businesses I work with that I'm an important person—that I'm noteworthy." She shrugs. "That's what convinces people in the fashion world."

We're driving through the streets of Milan's Montenapoleone district, past Armani and Versace and Bulgari and all the gleaming Italian luxury shops. "I'm very practical really," she says, pointing at her low-heeled black ankle boots on the car pedals. "I wear flats and jeans. I might wear some heels in the evening but I'm still very covered up and comfy." Under her thick turban, her hair is short. On a sunless, blustery afternoon, such practicality on the sidewalks is hard to find. There are bare legs and bare midriffs; a coatless woman in a short red dress tottering in heels; a huddle of friends standing with open jackets propped on their shoulders.

Nonini sighs, shifting down a gear as we hit congestion. "I don't need to be seductive. I need to go to meetings, have ideas, and get paid for them. Either I'm going to be valued because of what I say or because I have a nice ass—it can't be both." Her voice is quickening; she slaps the steering wheel. "If you conceive of yourself as an object and you behave like an object, then you're going to get treated like an object."

We pass a tram whose cars are covered in brightly colored ads for Hogan. "I did that," she says, pointing and suddenly cheerful. In 2015, she launched her H. Edge agency, specializing in brand experience and brand image. With her all-female team ("I have nothing against men, it just happened like that"), she's recently repositioned fashion brands including Hogan, Krizia and Faye. And she's brought her magic to corporations looking for her intuitive strategies—to Audi, to the Juventus soccer franchise, and to the Fidenza Village outlet complex, which she turned into a Las Vegas-like show for Christmas and which, at her behest, became pet-friendly this spring.

"To be a free thinker is truly the greatest luxury."

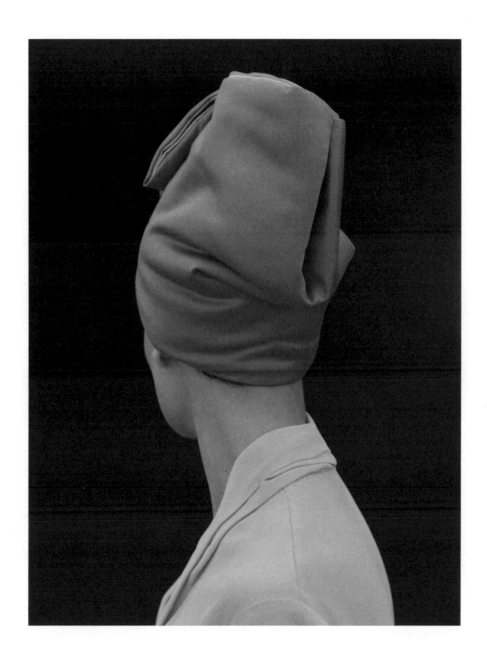

Left: Helen wears a suit by Krizia, a turban by Altalen and rings by Pomellato. Above: She wears a dress by Erika Cavallini and a turban by Altalen.

Nonini does not maintain an office. Preferring the vitality of public places, she conducts her daily research in the 19th-century library at Milan's Philological Society and her meetings at the café of the city's Triennale design museum. She also involves herself with sponsoring the arts so that she can be credible, she says, when persuading brands to do the same as part of her plan for them. "Art is much more relevant in our daily lives, and for these brands, than people imagine," she says.

Nonini's agency appears to be a world apart from the quixotic treasure hunts of her problem-solving days, but pragmatically it's another opportunity to capitalize on her wide-ranging knowledge, her intricate web of contacts, and her hyper-developed understanding of human desire. "When we create a plan for a brand, we imagine it first as a person—who would Hermès be, for example? She would be attentive, ironic, animated, tasteful. You need to understand a brand's personality to understand exactly what it is that's needed"—just as she formerly did with her bored rich clients.

We slide neatly into a petite parking space, but the car jerks once and my pen slips from my hand and falls between the parking brake and its plastic chassis. Nonini starts to feel around on the floor, then tugs at the chassis, sticks her fingers inside, and bangs it a few times, all in vain. The pen is lost forever, and a flicker of panic flashes across Nonini's face as she feels the imperative to problem solve. She grits her teeth: "I'll get you a pen."

Inside Altalen, we're greeted by owners Elena Todros and Antonina De Luca, in identical red and black striped tops. "Helen," they murmur as they stroke her arms and kiss her cheeks. Among the legions of wire hat stands and wooden shelves are framed pictures of Nonini. She wears birdlike turbans, her headdresses folded and pleated into soaring, winged creations, her expression direct and scorching. Meanwhile, in real life, by a bouquet of lilies and pussy willows, Nonini is rummaging through the drawers of the shop's counter.

"Don't you have any pens with caps?" she beseeches. Finally, Nonini hands me a bald Bic ballpoint. It's one of her practical substitutions and a definitive step down from my lost Japanese fine-point pen, but the problem is solved.

Decompressing, Nonini tries on the lime-green turban she'll match with a borrowed Missoni outfit for a dinner later that evening. Her connection to turbans is stylistic, not religious or traditional, but she tells me proudly that she feels justified in her choice—the turban was born in Iran, her grandfather's homeland.

Before we leave, Nonini pulls up a photo on her phone of the Suzuki sisters, eccentric Japanese twins with matching flamingo-colored bobs and coordinated pink furs, snapped on their way to the Gucci show. "Look at them! I had to photograph them—people need to pay attention to these two." The Altalen designers purr their approval.

We head off to Missoni. "People see me as some sort of trendsetter, but I'm not," Nonini insists as we arrive and slip between the clusters of journalists and PR people gathered in front of the show. "I'm simply someone capable of looking at reality from different viewpoints—of zooming in and zooming out. It's my outsider specialty." Consumed with understanding an ever-changing physical and social landscape, she has adopted a perspective of flexibility, of infinite inspection.

"To be a free thinker is truly the greatest luxury," she says, before a photographer leads her away to the photo op wall where, astonishingly, the Suzuki twins are waiting (apparently summoned by the Missoni team after spotting the pair on Nonini's Instagram account). They flank Nonini as the photographer takes their photo—a striking woman in a simple oversized knit cardigan and a high turban holding court.

Left: Helen wears a top and skirt by Gabriele Colangelo, shoes by Céline, turban by Altalen and jewelry from Pomellato.

Case Design

On an industrial estate near Mumbai's airport, a team of international architects and designers have found a way of alchemizing the city's chaotic spirit into something crisp, context-driven and beautiful. Words by *Mansi Choksi* & Photography by *Ariel Huber*.

Mumbai is a city that requires some measure of humor to survive. It's a place that fills you with optimism and the sense that you are in a rising part of the world, but it's also bursting with frustrations and creative subversions of the law. It has a brand of maddening chaos all its own.

"If you can't accept and adapt and go with that flow, you are constantly going to be frustrated," says Samuel Barclay, an American architect. We're sitting in the Case Design studio, an architecture and design practice he co-founded with Dutch architect Anne Geenen, inside an industrial complex in north Mumbai, beside a factory producing auto parts and a workshop making plastic cups. The studio suggests its own version of organized chaos. In the back room, carpenters and designers are at work creating miniature models of their projects to show at the Venice Biennale. Outside, an architect is studying the topography of a hillside in Indonesia, where Case Design is building a guesthouse. Geenen is making herself a cup of coffee. Barclay has just arrived, a motorcycle helmet in the crook of one elbow and his shirt drenched in sweat. "If you can actually see the chaos as an opportunity for a different way to work," Barclay continues, "then there are so many possibilities that immediately open up." Barclay and Geenen describe Case Design's architecture, design and interior projects as "a practice committed to exploring the design process through acts of making." I'm here to understand what that means.

At Case Design, every sketch, model, mock-up or piece of furniture is the product of an argument. I'm sitting on a wooden folding chair that was originally designed for a small cafe that doubled as a performance space. The chair went through numerous rounds of edits, mostly taking place over WhatsApp, and then at least 10 real-life versions. The final product incorporates the carpenter's suggestion to use traditional Indian joinery and the designer's idea to make a felt seat. "Everything becomes an opportunity for a conversation so that whatever is being discussed becomes better, but it also becomes an inclusive process that allows everybody to contribute their knowledge and feel invested in it," Barclay says.

Barclay moved to India in 2006, soon after graduating from the Southern California Institute of Architecture, to work with the architectural practice Studio Mumbai. By the time Barclay left that job, seven years later, he was managing director. Geenen, who studied at the University of Technology in Delft, had also briefly worked with Studio Mumbai and had heard about Barclay from carpenters she admired. At the time, in the midst of the global economic downturn and the daunting prospect of spending the winter in Europe, she was looking for a reason to stay in India. One evening, she cold-called Barclay. Four years later, they are the type of partners that finish each other's sentences.

Their first project together in 2013, as the newly minted Case Design, was a not-for-profit residential school for young women in Pune, a town outside Mumbai. The school was to be built on farmland, with a budget that more established practices would have considered laughable. "The challenge was to try to find solutions, despite limitations, to try to add something to the environment for students who would spend so much time there," Geenen says.

They decided to create buildings that were essentially concrete frames, planned around airy courtyards, walkways and terraces. The emphasis was on designing spaces that were economical, but that would feel familiar to the

CASEGOODS

by Harriet Fitch Little

In 2016, Case Design spun its architectural practice into a ready-made product line. Casegoods (by happy coincidence, the term is a synonym for hard furnishings in American English) comprises a range of lamps and furniture conceived by lead designer Paul Michelon. Items range in size from a conference-length table topped with thick marble, to the small, playful Rolling Round Light and a set of gently hollowed-out bowls carved from reclaimed rosewood, mahogany and teak. Attention to patination and grain is a signature across the otherwise diverse range.

students, many of whom would be living away from home for the first time. The floors were a mosaic made from scrap stone that the women would instantly recognize as something that they had seen in their own home, or in an aunt's or an uncle's. Cubbies outside classrooms were built from a stone that is considered so lowbrow that it is deemed fit for use only in hidden-away parts of Indian homes. The verandas were interspersed with *charpoys*, light bedsteads that are a fixture across rural India, so the space could turn into informal living rooms.

The school project became a learning experience for Barclay and Geenen. "I kept calling my carpenter, asking about the progress on the charpoys. I said, 'At least send me a picture. I need to know that the charpoys are going to arrive on time,'" Barclay says. "Between my bad Hindi and his English, I couldn't understand why it was taking so long." Finally, only days before the opening, a photo popped up on Barclay's phone. The charpoys were now strapped to the back of a public bus and were ready for dispatch. "I said, 'Why did it take so long?' And he says, 'The strings [which are strung across the bed frame] were being woven from torn saris.' When the men become too old to travel to job sites, they still want to do carpentry, but they do it from home. They sit together in some-

body else's courtyard and weave these charpoys."

Barclay becomes thoughtful as he talks about the rich and complicated personal histories that became woven into these pieces of furniture. "I'm not trained to think of charpoys as being an acceptable aesthetic. That's not what architecture school teaches you," he says. "But now I think it is a beautiful aesthetic. Right out of school, I would have made something sleek and cool and modern and completely inappropriate."

This philosophy that a building, home or a piece of furniture should carry a sense of time and place is apparent throughout Case Design's projects. Within four years, Case Design expanded to the Middle East, Africa and Southeast Asia, building structures in each location that would feel like they belonged there. In Zanzibar, Tanzania, they are building guest houses from a coral limestone that is ubiquitous across the island. In Hatta, United Arab Emirates, they are building a house from the soil on which it sits. And in Bali, Indonesia, they are building a home with bamboo.

The Mumbai apartment of wire mesh manufacturer Deven Shah and his wife, Bhavana, is an elegant example of Case Design's principles at work. The project began one evening in 2014: Geenen was working out of Barclay's living room, when a stranger showed up

at the door, out of breath. He kept asking for Barclay in Hindi, one ear attached to a cell phone. Finally, he thrust the phone at Geenen. On the other end of the line, Shah told her that he was looking for Barclay. He wanted him to design his home. Barclay and Geenen had three months to turn around a fully furnished apartment that had been ripped down to the floor.

When I walk into this apartment (pictured), I feel what it means to breathe a sense of belonging into a space. Today this home maps the histories, interests and aspirations of Deven and Bhavana. A picture-hanging system is mounted on the ceiling throughout the house so that Bhavana, a painter, can display her glorious art collection. There are Japanese-style sliding cupboard doors that include panels made from Deven's wire mesh fabric. The unpainted walls are plastered with nothing except cement, lime and marble powder because the couple wanted the house to feel more natural and less sterile. "Does it look like the photos?" Bhavana asks. "Because, you know, living here is a dream."

For Case Design, the simplicity and harmony of the apartment was the natural result of the personalization they aim to bring to every project. "We try to respond to the forces that are inherent in a context," Barclay says. "And then we adapt," Geenen adds.

Mumbai is the world's second most crowded city, a fact that makes Case Design's crisp, tranquil style particularly alluring to local residents.

THE EVOLUTION OF MATCHMAKING

TEXT:
HARRIET FITCH LITTLE

There was a time when matchmakers crossed deserts and climbed mountains to seek out candidates for marriage. These go-betweens juggled complex considerations of economic and social suitability—a process of "matching doors and windows" as it was euphemistically described in China. Now, computer algorithms can do the searching and sorting for us. Single people are able to access an abundance of potential soul mates with a few swipes. Why, then, in this era of seeming abundance, are offline matchmaking businesses thriving?

New York matchmaker Amy Van Doran looks like fashion designer Edna Mode from *The Incredibles*, only she's a few decades younger and her bobbed hair is not black but bright orange. Working out of a storefront in the East Village, Van Doran's job is to find love for a client list made up exclusively of women—most in their 40s—who each pay upwards of $15,000 for an entry in her vintage Rolodex.

It sounds like a stereotype 40 years out of date. And yet Van Doran is in high demand. More than that, she's considered cool. "When I first started out, matchmaking was something people were a little embarrassed about," she says. "Now I'm being invited to weddings, and people are telling their friends they're working with me."

Van Doran is walking through the East Village when we talk on the phone, and our conversation is punctuated with her greetings to the neighborhood passersby. (She often pulls New Yorkers in off the street if she thinks they look like a match for the "strong, successful women" on her books.) "I've always loved my clients, but every year they're becoming cooler," she says. "[They're] not people who are having trouble dating, [they're] people who are looking for a more curated experience."

Contrary to all expectations, this is a boom time for the matchmaking industry. Van Doran's Modern Love Club, which doubles as a gallery and mixer space, is often at capacity. Its charismatic founder claims that the number of similar businesses operating in New York has grown "from three to 300" since she started matchmaking a decade ago. This figure is surely exaggerated for persuasive effect (there

is no centralized registry for matchmakers, so no way of checking) but the trend is clear. In London, Caroline Brealey, founder of Matchmaker Academy (a training course for aspiring matchmakers) reports a similar surge: "I launched my matchmaking business just over six years ago, and I've seen many more matchmakers entering the market—partly because I bloody trained them," she says.

Meanwhile, in countries where matchmaking has always been the norm—often feeding into marriages that are arranged, or semi-arranged—the institution is bending but not disappearing. According to data from earlier in 2018, almost 90 percent of marriages in India are arranged by (or at least with the involvement of) parents—only a small decrease from the 95 percent of marriages that were arranged 15 years ago. "It's more like screened introductions," explains Canadian Reva Seth, whose book *First Comes Marriage* lays out the logic of this arrangement in positive terms. Seth says the Indian tradition persists in a modified form among its immigrant communities. "These couples definitely meet, usually with their families and then often alone for a coffee or quasi-date."

None of this is what the tech gurus predicted. Matchmaking is a business predicated on scarcity—of time and of options. When online dating became big business in the new millenium, and location-based apps like Tinder a decade after, it looked as if—to borrow a phrase from the American political scientist Francis Fukuyama—we had reached the end of matchmaking history. Some writers reported the shift online with hysterical panic. Writing in *Vanity*

Fair in 2015, Nancy Jo Sales branded it the "dating apocalypse": With endless opportunities for casual hookups, why would anyone commit to a relationship? Even those who weren't scandalized wondered where the change would leave the more traditional business of love matching, because why would anyone pay to outsource a service that they could do themselves? It would be like paying for takeout when you work in an office with a free cafeteria.

Matchmakers are keen to assert that whatever the reason for their current popularity, it is of a totally different stripe to that of their predecessors. "Matchmaking has historically been really problematic," says Van Doran, who touts her business as explicitly feminist in its approach. "I think a lot of things that are problematic about relationships began around the shift to the agricultural era. When people started owning land they started requiring monogamy and there started to be an ownership thing—you get your wife and you divide your land. That's when women started losing a lot of power."

But it is unfair to single out matchmakers as the problem, rather than the institution of marriage as a whole. Matchmakers are shape-shifters: They exist in societies with barriers to singles pairing up more naturally, and the form they take changes according to what exactly those barriers are. Often, it is distance. It is no coincidence that the most famous matchmaker in popular culture is Jewish—the *shadkhan* in *Fiddler on the Roof*, whose visits Tevye's five daughters greet with trepidation. From the 13th century to the 20th, Jewish *shtetls* were spread out across central and eastern Europe—often at considerable distance from one another. Matchmakers were vital lines of communication between the dispersed communities, and an emphasis on the need to ensure that matches were of equal education, social standing and income made the job of the shadkhan (fittingly, the word also means "stapler") a complicated one.

In China during the Qing dynasty, when large numbers of men were sent to settle remote provinces, matchmakers fanned out across the countryside to help them find wives. The 18th-century American pioneers did something similar, although they opted for more bureaucratic methods—having struck out west to occupy the interior, they would advertise for wives back on the East Coast to follow them.

Europeans generally believe that the 18th-century Enlightenment signaled a fundamental break with the past in thinking about love and marriage. Tradition was out; romantic love was in, along with skepticism, individualism and a new faith in the scientific method. But Clara Wollburg, an academic who has written at length about the shifting sands of matchmaking, argues that there was no sudden moment when singles upturned traditional considerations such as class in choosing their partner. After the Enlightenment, she writes, "marriage remained an economic unit often entered into because of societal or economic pressure... It was only in the 1970s that such constraints gradually diminished in most of Europe and the United States and marriage could be a 'personal relationship between two freely consenting adults.'"

But—and here's the rub—Wollburg also notes that it was at exactly this moment that the role of the professional matchmaker resurfaced via introduction agencies, singles ads, early computer dating and television shows. The ability to choose a "love match" had made a lot of things easier, but it had also opened a Pandora's box of romantic options. Rather than rooting out hard-to-find matches in a situation

of scarcity, the job of the matchmaker was now to whittle down an overwhelmingly long list of potential mates.

As with most puzzles of the mind and heart, the 20th-century's best and brightest turned to science for answers. The belief that finding a perfect match is just an algorithm away is one we've bought into with unswerving devotion for at least 100 years. In the 1920s, the American journal *Science and Invention* ran a fanciful piece suggesting ways in which machines might help to determine long-term compatibility. There were four elements: a test for physical attraction (measuring the pulse); a test for empathy (one half of the pair would have blood drawn, and the reaction of the other monitored); a nervous reaction test (a gun was fired and the examiner would make a note of who jumped in shock); and an odor test wherein one partner sat in a box and the other sniffed the smell of them through a tube. (Perhaps surprisingly, this last principle is the one back in fashion: Companies including Pheramor and Instant Chemistry now offer to match couples using DNA samples, their logic based on the fact that people are attracted to the smell of partners whose pheromones suggest a different immune system to their own.)

But the *Science and Invention* tests could never have been scaled. What was needed was mass data processing to sift through the sea of singletons. Computers and questionnaires provided the answer. Long before dating sites were in operation, their principles were pioneered by students at several Ivy League universities. Beginning in the early 1960s, they tried their luck feeding data submitted by young college students through enormous IBM computers that weighed several tons and looked like complex mixing decks. The questions they asked were preference-based, sometimes devised by marriage counselors and sometimes by the students themselves. "Do you like pets in the house?" was one of the key questions according to celebrity marriage counselor Paul Popenoe

(also a eugenicist and advocate of compulsory sterilization). The students were more mischievous, adding questions that probed the users' views on sex before marriage.

Over the last half-century, the programs have become infinitely more sophisticated. There are more than 7,500 online dating sites in the world, each of them using complicated algorithms to match partners not just on shared preferences but also complementary traits (the "opposites attract" philosophy of romance), life outlook and location. EHarmony —the US-based dating behemoth—encourages users to complete a 149-part survey measuring 29 elements of compatibility before they begin the matching process.

And yet, earlier this year eHarmony UK was forbidden from calling its matchmaking service "scientifically proven," with critics arguing that despite its enormously complicated handling of data, there was no compelling evidence that it offers users a better chance of finding lasting love than other dating strategies. The chairman of the UK Advertising Standards Authority ruled that the ads on the London Underground telling commuters that "It's time science had a go at love" were a "new form of fake news."

The eHarmony results are repeated across the board. (And eHarmony itself accounts for four percent of marriages in the US, a country where 20 percent of current relationships begin online.) Although online dating sites work in that they give people access to an enormous pool of potential partners, evidence shows that they are scarcely better than randomized matching at the business of pairing people up. Eli Finkel, the Northwestern University professor who published groundbreaking research to this effect in 2012, suggests that algorithms fail because only a negligible fraction of relationship satisfaction is as the result of shared interests (studies suggest it is as low as 0.5 percent). Personality is hardly more indicative: According to a 2010 study of married couples in

"The ability to choose a 'love match' opened a Pandora's box of romantic options. Rather than rooting out hard-to-find matches in a situation of scarcity, the job of the matchmaker was now to whittle down an overwhelmingly long list of potential mates."

the UK, Germany and Australia, having similar personality traits only accounts for a six percent boost to relationship satisfaction.

Added to these unpromising findings, we are not prone to truth-telling online. "Algorithms themselves can throw up the odd surprise and serendipitous love match, of course, but they're relying on your data—how honest are you really being?" says Justin Myers, a writer who blogs about dating under the pseudonym The Guyliner and whose first book, *The Last Romeo*, was published earlier this year. The book tells the tale of a gay man looking for love online, who starts out innocently optimistic about his chances of finding a boyfriend but eventually becomes bitter and hardened by the experience. "Online dating has turned many of us into consummate if harmless liars—presenting a social media-esque, filtered version of ourselves," says Myers. "That's usually the undoing of many relationships forged on them."

But what's the alternative? According to the research amassed by Finkel and others, the best way of predicting compatibility is to watch two people interact, because communication style and conflict resolution matter more than personality in determining whether a relationship could last. And that's where traditional matchmakers contend they have the edge.

"I don't think the intuition is there if you're not meeting both parties," says Van Doran. "The reason I'm good at my job is I've interviewed 7,000 people." Van Doran says she can get a good sense of what people really want, and how they will interact, by examining them closely when she meets them. She is interested in a romantic strain of attachment theory—the idea that the relationships we form with our parents when we're young influence the way we interact in relationships in the future. And she believes that by quizzing potential matches on their childhood attachments (as well as more prosaic questions) she can get a sense of compatibility that goes beyond mere likes and dislikes. "There's this moment where I sense a

match and slam my hands down on the desk and point," Van Doran explains excitedly. "It doesn't happen that often but when it does, [the couple in question] ends up getting married. Last year that happened four times."

Fatigue with online dating has helped the matchmakers in that it has driven romantic hopefuls offline. The challenge that comes with it is that they are no longer operating in a situation of scarcity: People may not be finding the *right* person via Tinder, but they're painfully aware that an enormous number of people are out there. "I think that online dating has given people a lot of really bad habits," says Van Doran. "People have become a lot more critically engaged with what they're looking for rather than what they're bringing to the table." Brealey says the same is true in the UK: "People think too far ahead too soon. We'll match a client with someone who is originally from a different country and they'll say, 'What if they wanted to go back to their country at some point? I can't do it,'" she recalls. "I say, 'Calm down; all you're doing is meeting them for a glass of wine.'"

This problem is called the "paradox of choice": When presented with multiple options, our ability to choose between them decreases and we feel less satisfied overall with the range available. According to *First Comes Marriage* author Seth, arranged marriages are for the most part successful (divorce rates are low, and after a few years the couples are as satisfied as those who made love matches) because those who go into them do so with a belief that they're in it for the long haul. "The most relevant lesson from those of us in arranged marriages is to have realistic expectations both from our partners and the institution of marriage," says Seth. "In my book, I talk about the damaging myth of the soul mate and how it has made it so much harder for people to find happiness in their relationships." It may sound like a cold-hearted approach, but the modern matchmakers agree. "Arranged marriages are focused on 'How do I make this marriage

work?'" says Van Doran. "It's much less egotistical. It's treating it like a well-run business or something."

Looking to the future, Brealey worries that her industry will be shaken by the number of big dating sites that are now offering human matchmakers as add-ons to their online services. EHarmony, for example, has launched a $5,000-a-year option to have a real person help you sift through potential dates. "They're adding on exclusive matchmaking and not charging as much as a typical matchmaker would and people know the brand," says Brealey. "That's a big discussion at the moment. What are they about? What are they going to do?" Another likely disruption will come through virtual reality technology. If widespread, it would allow couples to achieve that all-important "face-to-face" time without schlepping across the city to go on a date. But both Van Doran and Brealey seem confident that their offices won't be shuttering anytime soon. "I think there's this nostalgia for more curated experiences—like artisan-made whiskey or something like that," Van Doran says cheerfully.

And, Justin Myers points out, whatever happens with the technology it's unlikely that matchmakers will disappear entirely from popular consciousness because the process is so fun to consume vicariously as entertainment. Dating game shows established a firm foothold in TV scheduling in the 1980s and haven't relinquished it. "We believe in the Hollywood ending," says Myers, who writes a popular blog in which he dissects *The Guardian's* weekly Blind Date column. "While dating itself is like staggering from one motorway pileup to another, the art of matchmaking—of imagining love blossoming, and watching those first steps—is quite satisfying."

"Plus, when it all goes wrong, we love to dissect the gory details," he adds. "It's like a modern version of being a *tricoteuse* at the guillotine, but with two-for-one cocktails and dick pics."

D

E

Photography by Pelle Crépin & Styling by David Nolan

P

Inspired by the painter Pierre Soulages, an exploration of the impossible luminosity of layered black textures.

T

H

Above: Betty wears a coat and knitwear by Pringle of Scotland, a dress by Margaret Howell and shoes by A.P.C. Right: Raith wears a shirt by Phoebe English.

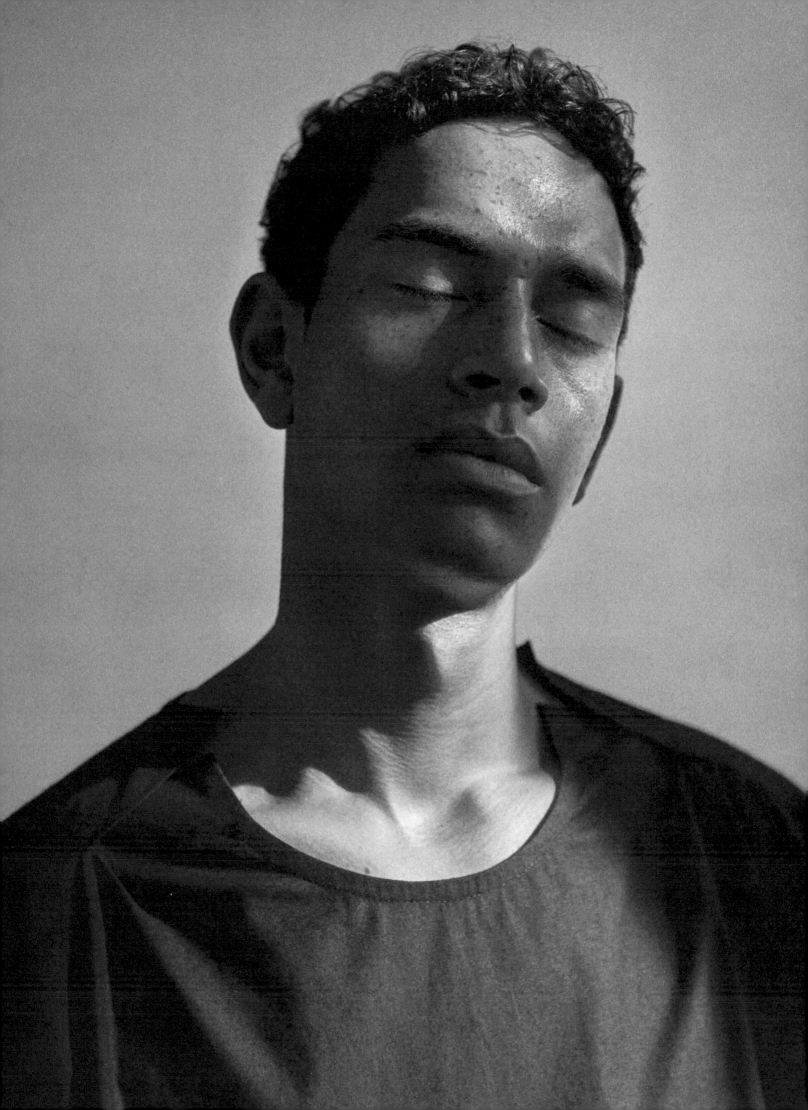

Left: Betty wears a dress and shoes by Simone Rocha. Below: Raith wears a tuxedo suit by Lanvin.

Left: Raith wears trousers by Gieves & Hawkes, shoes by George Cleverley and socks by Pantherella. Below: He wears a coat by Ermenegildo Zegna, a shirt by JW Anderson and a knit by Margaret Howell.

Left: Raith wears Anderson & Sheppard head-to-toe. Above: Betty wears a dress by Shushu/Tong

Raith and Betty both wear knitwear by Acne Studios and trousers by Skiim.

Day in the Life:
Rinus Van de Velde

As a teenager, *Rinus Van de Velde* dreamed of following in the footsteps of his avant-garde art heroes. The only problem? He quickly realized he was more of a routine-loving homebody than a rebellious hedonist. In Antwerp, we meet the wild child who never was—and hear how art allows him to lead a double life. Words by *Pip Usher* & Photography by *Marsý Hild Þórsdóttir*.

Back when Rinus Van de Velde was an ordinary teenager living in an ordinary village in rural Belgium, he saw something on television that would change what happened next. It was a biopic of Jean-Michel Basquiat, the prodigiously talented *enfant terrible* of New York's '80s art scene. "I realized that, apart from all the normality I saw [here], this was also a way that you could lead your life," Van de Velde, who now lives in Antwerp, recalls. Born to a teacher mother and an engineer father, he had never met a bona fide artist before. Captivated by this televised portrayal of a tortured creative, he began to pretend to be such a man himself. In his bedroom, he'd quietly practice drawing—all the while fantasizing about the other, more exciting, life that he felt certain was out there waiting for him. He visited Paris' Museum of Modern Art and queued for three hours to see an exhibition on fauvist art. After that, it was decided: He too would join the iconoclastic ranks of art's avant-garde. "There was always a longing to be somebody like an artist or a rock star," he says.

In many ways, Van de Velde has accomplished what he set out to do. The 34-year-old is a leading figure in Belgium's contemporary art scene, with his work represented by galleries in Berlin and Antwerp. His large-scale charcoal drawings, many of which are self-portraits, show scenes of epic heroism and far-flung travels. In one, a wild-haired man hangs suspended by his feet with ropes as he daubs paints on a canvas in the center of a studio strewn with artistic trappings. Another depicts four hardy men aboard a tiny boat with a foam-tipped wave threatening to curl over the side.

In this hypermasculine world, gallantry and adventure go hand in hand and death lurks just over the next wave. It's precisely the unruliness that Van de Velde dreamed of from his bedroom several decades ago. And yet it's also diametrically opposed to his current real-life existence. "It's an autobiography, but a fictionalized autobiography," he explains from the home he shares with his girlfriend and their two-year-old twins. "For example, when I want to make a drawing of me in the jungle, I would never go to the actual jungle but I would stage one here in my studio."

Herein lies the paradox of Van de Velde; he's a dreamer and a free spirit who doesn't actually like to travel and who lives by a rigid routine. Each day he's in the studio by 8 a.m., and every lunchtime he joins friends at the same restaurant nearby. Sunday nights are spent at the

Van de Velde's conceptual approach is reminiscent of post-impressionist painter Henri Rousseau, who was famous for painting exotic jungles and animals that he had never seen in real life.

"I can't cope with total freedom. I need restrictions."

movies. Even his monochromatic charcoal drawings are constructed within strict parameters. "I can't cope with total freedom," he admits, laughing. "If you put me in a studio with a lot of paint and a lot of color, I would get confused and frustrated because there's too much possibility. I need restrictions."

This inherent set of contradictions has been the defining feature of Van de Velde's biography. After graduating from Antwerp's St. Lucas School of Arts in 2006, he remained in the city, attracted to its cheap studio space and concentrated creative community. After a while, he found that his life had become entrenched there: close friends, a girlfriend. But still he found himself enamored with those teenage dreams of adventure.

"I started fantasizing about this life I didn't have because I was always in my studio, which is a bit of a white cube," he explains. "So, I started to invent this story, or these memories which never happened, and it enabled me to stay in my studio, where I like it most, and still think about experiences which I could have had."

Alone in his studio, TV murmuring in the background, Van de Velde translated these fantasies into art. Working from a database of images collated from film stills, newspaper clippings, history books and more, he decided to deliberately ignore any text that accompanied them. Instead, he envisioned his own narrative. What was happening in each picture? And what role did he play in it? From there, he'd begin to draw, often inserting himself into the action as the floppy-haired, hollow-eyed protagonist. With each imaginative character, a fresh identity was assumed and a new experience had—from the safety and seclusion of his studio. "It's all about pretending, not about reality," he says.

As his body of work developed, Van de Velde progressed into building his own sets, transforming the studio space into whatever fantasy had captured his imagination. His latest exhibition, held at the Tim Van Laere Gallery in Antwerp, was based loosely on the rip-roaring escapades of Tintin in the graphic novel *Prisoners of the Sun*. But instead of Tintin he inserted his own alter ego, a forgotten abstract expressionist who went by the name of Robert Rino. Kidnapped by a collector, Rino was being forced to create art against his will as he waited in the jungle for rescue. In addition to his usual large-scale charcoal compositions, Van de Velde filled the gallery with pop-colored tropical plants, the open trunk of a pistachio-green car and wreckage from an aircraft that had nosedived into the center of the room. All were fashioned from wood and painted cardboard, lending a zany, cartoon-esque dimension to the

more somber scenes depicted in the drawings hung across the walls. "A lot of the time, I think it's more interesting to fantasize about going to a jungle than to actually go there," he explains. "I don't like to travel that much and, when I do, I really don't get why people are traveling the world to learn about it. You can also learn a lot from books or just by thinking about how it would be to be at a certain place."

Having a fictional alter ego such as Robert Rino also allows him to experiment with appropriation art. Van de Velde showed a collection of work at a gallery in Amsterdam that was based around the fabricated experiences of Rino. "I made charcoal drawings showing his life and his career. And I also made some fake abstract expressionist works inspired [by] de Kooning and Twombly which were [exhibited as] original Robert Rino in the show," he says. Although his own art has always been markedly different from that of the postwar painters, Van de Velde used Rino as a tool to connect with a transformative period in modern art's history. "I liked the fact that when I was making these original Robert Rino works my whole practice was kind of split up and became schizophrenic," he says.

Such untethered imagination—coupled with a highly distinctive drawing style—invites viewers into Van de Velde's universe. From there, the inclusion of text draws them further into the drama unfolding on the canvas. As a teenager, he remembers arriving in Paris and looking at paintings with only a small plaque to guide him. In his own work, he has decided to lift the artist's shroud so that his drawings carry clear meaning and emotional clout. "I think the best art is very individual," he says. "It's so related to the artist's persona."

This year, Van de Velde plans to collaborate with friends on a film that will expand upon his charcoal drawings and his sculptures to create an even more immersive experience. It's a careful, deliberate deepening of the oeuvre he's developed over the years and the next chapter in this wild fictional autobiography that's emerging—even as his own role as leading man becomes ever-more family-oriented.

"Everyone has this internal image of themselves, or this goal of what they want to be. They don't actually want it. They want things to stay the same," he says. For him, that means an afternoon tennis lesson, time with the kids, and a little more drawing before bed. It's certainly a different vision of freedom from the one embodied by Basquiat. And yet, to Van de Velde, those quiet, structured hours stretching ahead make for "a perfect day."

Van de Velde's signature style—swirling charcoal lines that melt into one another—unifies his otherwise eclectic oeuvre.

LA DOLCE VITA

Warm skin, gelato and the rustle of cypress leaves: Postcards from an Italian summer.

Photography by Annie Lai & Styling by Kingsley Tao

Above: Daniel wears a shirt by Comme des Garçons, a tie by Calvin Klein and a jacket by Xander Zhou.

Right: Layla wears a jacket by Toga Archives, a dress by Merchant Archive and a hat by Off-White.

Above: Layla wears a shirt by Rejina Pyo, a skirt by Molly Goddard and earrings by Paula Knorr. Right: Daniel wears a suit by Chin Menswear, shoes by Xander Zhou, a tie by Lanvin, a belt by Margaret Howell and a necklace by Goods by Goodhood.

Above: Daniel wears a jacket, trousers and shoes by Xander Zhou, a shirt by Comme
des Garçons and a belt by Margaret Howell. Right: He wears a jacket by Chin Menswear and a shirt by JW Anderson.

Archive:
Grace Kelly

Actress, princess, icon, enigma: Hitchcock's most famous blonde boomeranged between social conformity and hardheaded rebellion over the course of her too-short life. Writer *Katie Calautti* delves into the archives to try and better understand Hollywood's "snow-covered volcano."

When 18-year-old Grace Kelly convinced her parents to let her move from Philadelphia to New York City to pursue her dream of acting, it was not with their glowing endorsement. "It's not as if she's going to *Hollywood*, after all," said her mother. "It'll never amount to anything," her father agreed dismissively. This was not the first time, nor would it be the last time, that the Kellys underestimated their daughter. Their disapproval was the mortar with which the bricks of her life were laid, and with which Kelly would go on to fashion a literal palace.

In the six years between 1950 and 1956, Kelly starred in 11 movies and became one of Hollywood's most enduring icons. So much has been said of the Oscar-winning actress, Alfred Hitchcock muse, and eventual Princess of Monaco in the 67 years since she burst onto the scene that to construct a sound characterization of her is, as reporter Pete Martin once wrote, "Like trying to wrap up 115 pounds of smoke." Kelly's life, like her persona, was a showcase of duality—an endless tug-of-war between social conformity and rebellion. The "snow-covered volcano," as Hitchcock famously described her, simmered for 52 short years.

Kelly was raised wanting for nothing—at least, not in the material sense. Her father, John B. "Jack" Kelly Sr., had found fame in the early 1920s as an Olympic athlete (he was the first rower to win three gold medals), then earned millions of dollars through his family's bricklaying business. Her mother, Margaret, a former model and competitive swimmer, was the first woman to teach physical education at the University of Pennsylvania.

The shy and sickly third of four children, Kelly was the sweet-natured, imaginative yin to her athletic, outgoing brother and sisters' yang. "My family told me they thought I was practically born with a cold," Kelly once said. Her mother ruled the roost with an iron fist, and her father judged his children's success based on their athletic prowess. "We were always competing," recalled Kelly. "Competing for everything, competing for love."

Her upbringing taught her to build a protective barrier between her outer and inner worlds—the early creation of that Grace Kelly mystique so many still marvel over. As her *To Catch a Thief* co-star Cary Grant said, when Kelly confronted adversity, "She'd just enclose herself in what my wife at the time used to call her 'plastic egg'—that she could see out of, but you couldn't get in."

Kelly moved to New York in 1947 to pursue acting, where mention of her Pulitzer Prize-winning uncle George Kelly earned her an audition at the American Academy of Dramatic Arts. "I think most of what went on after that was thanks to herself, that she had a great look and she definitely personified that cool blonde,"

Even early in her career, Kelly was strong-willed. She refused Hitchcock's request to wear "falsies" on the set of *Rear Window*.

"I was hired to be an actress, not a personality for the press."

says Jonathan Kuntz, film historian and UCLA lecturer. After a successful stint as a model, her ticket to Hollywood came in early 1950 when she screen-tested for a movie called *Taxi*. She didn't get the part, but the reel eventually made its way to her future directors John Ford and Alfred Hitchcock.

After a rather underwhelming two-minute-long debut in 1951's *Fourteen Hours*, 1952's *High Noon* was a notable upgrade. It positioned 23-year-old Kelly opposite legendary actor Gary Cooper, who was almost 30 years her senior—an immense age difference that would become standard for her leading men. "Kelly was so rarely paired with men her own age," film historian and *You Must Remember This* podcast creator Karina Longworth notes. "To the point where, in hindsight, it feels like the entirety of her persona pre-royalty was wrapped up in being the young object of desire for an older man."

The enticement of acting alongside Clark Gable and Ava Gardner on location in Kenya for Ford's 1953 film *Mogambo* lured Kelly into what she considered the indentured servitude of Hollywood: a seven-year contract with Metro-Goldwyn-Mayer Studios (MGM). She astonished her agents and MGM executives by requesting alterations to the paperwork, requiring every other year off so she could take on theater work, and maintaining her primary residence in New York. This would be the first of many contentious dealings with her studio.

The role in *Mogambo* earned Kelly a Golden Globe for best supporting actress, solidifying her rising star status; now she officially had the attention of Hitchcock. Kelly asserted her will on his sets from the very start, telling the exacting director that her *Dial M for Murder* character would

never put on an elaborate robe to answer the phone in the middle of the night—she'd simply do so in her nightgown. Hitchcock relented, and after that, gave her a great deal of freedom to dictate her wardrobe in their next two film collaborations.

MGM studio head Dore Schary often fed her lightweight roles in fluffy films, but Kelly always dug her heels in, saying, "If anybody starts using me as scenery, I'll return to New York." (After all, unlike most struggling actors, Kelly didn't need their money: She had a trust fund granted by her father on her 21st birthday.) She was equally stubborn about giving interviews. "I was hired to be an actress, not a personality for the press," Kelly once said.

Her all-around obstinacy earned her a short suspension from MGM in early 1955—so the freshly Oscar-nominated actress made two unprecedented moves: Without consulting her PR agents, she informed the press of MGM's action and went on vacation in Jamaica with her sister Peggy. Kelly invited photographer Howell Conant along, and Kelly and Conant proceeded to take spontaneous, intimate images the likes of which had never been seen in glamour-obsessed Hollywood. The goal was to present Kelly as a human being—the opposite of the treatment she was getting in Los Angeles.

Considering her disdain for the press, it's ironic that a publicity stunt during Kelly's visit to the 1955 Cannes Film Festival changed the course of her life. The movie editor of *Paris Match* magazine roped Kelly into a 30-minute photo op at Prince Rainier's palace in Monaco, a small principality bordering France. The single 32-year-old monarch, like Kelly, was very much in the news at the time—if Rainier did not produce

Kelly's parents approved of her marriage to Rainier, because it assured their social standing in Philadelphia society.

an heir, Monaco would revert to French control.

Once Kelly returned to the States, Rainier wrote to thank her for her visit. The two began corresponding regularly, and found they had much in common—Rainier, too, had an unhappy, lonely childhood and at times felt burdened by his very public position. Six months later, Rainier visited the United States with his priest and doctor in tow, set on asking Kelly to marry him. When asked in an interview, "If you were to marry, what kind of girl do you have in mind?" His response was, "I don't know—the best." That is what Kelly's parents had always raised her to be—and despite all her career success, it was with this match that she, at last, earned their attention.

Three days after meeting the Kellys, Rainier proposed. After submitting to an exam from Rainier's doctor that confirmed Kelly could bear children, Rainier gave her a 10.47-carat diamond, which she wore as her character's engagement ring in what would be her last movie, *High Society*.

So why did Kelly leave her hard-won career—within which she'd carved out an unusual amount of autonomy—for an even more structured life in Monaco's palace? "I don't want my wife to work," Rainier told the press. And against the backdrop of 1950s society, being a wife and a mother was still the ultimate accomplishment. Kelly also saw her makeup call times being bumped an hour earlier—a sign that the 26-year-old was already aging out of Hollywood. And a friend recalled that she doubted her abilities as an actress and felt there was nowhere for her to go but down after her Oscar win for *The Country Girl*.

In April 1956, Kelly prepared for what the media had dubbed "the wedding of the century" when she sailed with friends and family on the USS Constitution to Monaco. She carried with her four massive trunks and 56 pieces of luggage, along with her wedding dress—a gift from MGM—stored in a steel box resembling a coffin as a ruse to throw off reporters.

The macabre metal-encased wedding dress was an unhappy foreshadowing. Royal life proved a bad trade for Kelly—she was terribly lonely and isolated from the start. "I became princess before I had much time to imagine what it would be," Kelly said. Studying to be royalty was unlike any of her acting jobs—she could skirt convention in Hollywood, but in Monaco old rules reigned. And the adjustment to palace life was hard: Rainier was often preoccupied with affairs of state, and until she learned French there was a language barrier between her and her staff. Even the births of her three children couldn't completely fill the void left by her career.

In 1960, Kelly's father was diagnosed with terminal cancer. After the princess left his Philadelphia bedside, her personal secretary, Phyllis Blum, recalled that Kelly broke down in tears—it was the first time she'd seen the princess cry. With the death of John B. Kelly, the man who had greeted his daughter's 1955 Oscar win by telling the press that, "Of the four children, she's the last one I'd expected to support me in my old age," the snow-topped volcano began its thaw. Photographer Eve Arnold visited Monaco to work on a CBS documentary in 1962, and recalled, "I got the distinct feeling that Kelly felt trapped." That same year, Kelly's shot at coming out of retirement arrived when Hitchcock offered her the title role in *Marnie*. She was overjoyed, and perhaps because he now had his heir, Rainier allowed her to accept. But as Donald Spoto writes in his biography of Kelly, she reneged when she learned she was pregnant. Two weeks later, she miscarried. It was never made public, so the official reason was given as an angry outcry from the Monegasque people, who supposedly didn't want to see their princess kissing another man. Kelly never returned to Hollywood.

Rainier and Kelly's relationship became more distant in the 1970s. Kelly often escaped with her daughters to Paris for months at a time, and in 1976 she joined the board of 20th Century Fox, telling a friend, "It gets me away from Monaco at least four times a year." She also began wandering the mountains of Monaco collecting flowers, which she eventually turned into art and exhibited. The new hobby puzzled those close to her. "Here was one of the most vital women in the world, and she's

"I became princess before I had much time to imagine what it would be."

Photograph: Philippe Le Tellier/Paris Match/Getty Images

"'I've been accused of being cold, snobbish, distant," Kelly once said. "Those who know me well know that I'm nothing of the sort."

"She dreamed about the days when no one would care about her and she could be a bag lady..."

making pressed flower collages?" said her friend Rupert Allan. She began drinking heavily by the late 1970s, and friends observed she was struggling with depression.

On September 13, 1982, Kelly and her youngest daughter, Stephanie, left the family's country home for Monaco in their 1972 Rover 3500. She had an appointment with her couturier, and loaded some dresses that needed altering into the back seat. Because the car was crowded, she drove herself and left their usual chauffeur behind. Kelly never liked to drive, and the winding mountain roads on the way to Monaco were especially difficult to navigate. A truck driver witnessed her car swerving,

then speeding up and flying over a cliff. The car bounced upside down, rolled several times and then came to a stop on its roof.

Stephanie suffered a hairline fracture to her neck; Kelly was unresponsive. The palace issued an early alert that the princess only had a broken leg, but it was later revealed that she had experienced a massive stroke while driving, and another brain injury in the crash. Kelly was taken off life support the following day. She was just 52 years old. All of Monaco—and Hollywood—grieved.

Kelly's friend Robert Dornhelm recalled, "She always told me that she dreamed about the days when no one would care about her

and she could be a bag lady wandering through the Metro in Paris." It was never to be; even 36 years after she was laid to rest, an internet search of Kelly yields a photo of her lying in state in her coffin. The photographers that plagued her throughout her life refused to relent beyond it. (Though one notably did: The only time that Howell Conant did not pack his camera for a flight to Monaco was the trip to Kelly's funeral.)

It seems everything happened early for Grace Kelly: Her pain, her fame, her marriage, her disenchantment, and her death. As Kelly herself once told Spoto, "The idea of my life as a fairy tale is itself a fairy tale."

After a life lived on camera, Kelly's funeral in 1982 was broadcast live around the world.

114 — 176

Hair

D

I

A

N

A

Supreme: A short history of Diana Ross' hair.

Words by Pamela K. Johnson

Previous Page: Photograph by Harry Langdon/Getty Images, Left Photograph: CBS Photo Archive/Getty Images

Throughout the 1960s, the Supremes topped the charts with a barrage of hits, from "Baby Love" to "My World is Empty Without You" to "I Hear a Symphony."

They also dazzled audiences with their head-to-toe style. Motown Records' premiere girl group didn't have the hundred-thousand-dollar glam squads today's stars have up their sleeves, but Diana Ross, Mary Wilson and Florence Ballard made do. They relied on curling irons and jars of hair goo, along with an extensive wig collection. If their shoes were a different color than their fleet of slinky evening gowns, they would dye them to match.

Ross, the rising star of the trio, went on to pursue solo singing and acting careers. But through her many seasons in the spotlight, she hasn't been allowed to have bad hair days. Whether she's come off a long flight, been battling the flu or nursing a broken heart, her fans have always expected her to step out looking like a million dollars—with interest.

In her memoir, *Secrets of a Sparrow*, Ross writes that the quest for low-budget perfection came naturally to her, dating back to her early years in Detroit's Brewster-Douglass Housing Projects. "I had always been good at doing hair," she recalls. "I remember that my mother had been adept at using the curling irons, and I must have picked it up from her." Ross would place the metal implements atop a fire on the stove, and practice on her own hair, "Twist[ing] and turn[ing] those curlers and hav[ing] them literally dancing in my hands." Then—once the Supremes started singing as a trio—she began to make over bandmates Wilson and Ballard, using styles cadged from magazines and TV shows. "Another part of our signature look was the beautiful gowns we wore," she writes. "Even as teenagers, we had a sense of sophistication that made us stand out from other performers."

Juliette Harris, my co-editor on *Tenderheaded: A Comb-Bending Collection of Hair Stories*, remembers the Supremes' early days from her own childhood in Virginia. "Whenever they would play a major city, the marketing and promotion people would contact the local radio station and let the kids know," says Harris. "The Supremes were arriving in two hours

Growing up in Detroit, Ross' family called her the "wiggle tail" because of her seemingly boundless energy.

"In almost every photo session, I tried to change my hair."

at the Richmond airport, and I got my mother to take me. They were dressed very chic: heels and stockings, bouffant wigs, and they carried round hat boxes." Harris asserts that instead of hats, those boxes were actually carefully layered with wigs.

The Supremes sported the hairstyles of the era: the beehive, the bob, and the flip. At the time, Harris says, she grooved to their music but never copied their hair: "I admired that they—and [jazz singer] Nancy Wilson—were young black women who were being portrayed as glamorous," she says, "but I always wanted to look more bohemian." But over the years, Ross has rocked all the looks: From big and poufy to face-framing sleek; from afros and braids to pixie cuts and wedges; from long to short to curly and straight—and occasionally with oodles of ornaments. "In almost every photo session, I tried to change my hair," Ross reveals in *Secrets of a Sparrow*. And by changing her hair, she means (mostly) changing her wig.

Betty Brandly, a hairstylist in Long Beach, California, remembers a time when black women got dinged for wearing what was then referred to as store-bought hair: "People would point if they knew you had a wig on, or a piece in your hair," says Brandly, who owns Twist N Shout salon. "Ross helped bridge that gap, that stigma of not being able to wear anything that wasn't your hair."

Mikki Taylor, author of the new book *Editor in Chic: How to Style and Be Your Most Empowered Self,* agrees. "Ross lives in a judgment-free zone. That's what gives her a sense of vibrancy," she says. "If you want to wear 22 inches of curly hair, shave your head or put on two pairs of false eyelashes, you're living the one life that belongs to you!"

Taylor has styled Ross on several occasions. The first time was in 1982, when Taylor was on staff as *Essence*'s beauty editor and helmed the publication's cover shoots. She recalls one shoot with Ross, for a holiday issue, set around New York landmarks. They set up a scene in Times Square, and people began to recognize the woman at the center of it all. Initially, they milled about, but then began to close in. Taylor worried that the crush of fans might not only unnerve Ross but also ruin the photos. "Someone else would have been scared, but Miss Ross was perfectly comfortable with the people," Taylor recalls. "They're all right, it's all right," she assured Taylor. On the cover, Ross' wet curls evoked "a raw, different kind of glamour," says Taylor, now editor at large at *Essence*. "You didn't see wet hair on covers back then."

For many black women, water is a hairstyle's sworn enemy. Black women rarely wash-and-go; we wash, style, dry and ride it out for a week or two—or, yikes, three—before rinsing and repeating. So to Brandly, the Long Beach hairstylist, Ross deserves bonus points for being a swimmer: "She's not afraid of water. She likes to swim, and I do, too. She was on the swim team in high school," Brandly says. "She

Photograph: Harry Langdon/Getty Images

Ross once revealed that her career strategy was to think about where she wanted to be in 20 years' time, and then figure out how to get there.

was doing it way back then, and that to me says a lot."

If you lay all the diva's moments end to end, the one that would take center stage involves Ross and a ton of water. It was the free concert that she attempted to give to nearly 450,000 fans on Central Park's Great Lawn in July 1983—only Mother Nature did not warn her that thunder, lightning, and more than two inches of rain were also on the bill that night.

It was a stressful evening. As Ross tried to outshine the rain, TV audiences around the country watched her get drenched by the flash storm—and fretted over the wired microphone in her hand, and the electrical equipment surrounding her. "Everybody was worried," says Taylor, "but she is fearless. When she was singing 'Ain't no mountain high enough… no wind, no rain, can stop me, babe' you couldn't ask for a better metaphor for

being your authentic self. Anybody else would've been ushered off the stage by bodyguards, but she stayed till everyone was out of the park safely, and the lights were out."

For a stretch of years in the 1970s, Ross nabbed attention for a string of feature films: *Lady Sings the Blues*, *Mahogany* and *The Wiz*. The last of these was the least successful in terms of critical acclaim, perhaps because it had to stand up to the classic source material, *The Wizard of Oz*. *The Wiz*, like its predecessor, was about a girl named Dorothy who is blown far from home, and who can only find her way back through a tortuous path that involves gleaning key life lessons. In a short afro and simple white dress, Ross, then 34, played Dorothy as a schoolteacher from Harlem, amid an ensemble cast that included Michael Jackson as the Scarecrow and Richard Pryor

as the Wiz. *Time* magazine was not impressed: "Banks will not back a big film unless the star is someone even a banker has heard of," lamented critic John Skow. "Thus, when you want to cast a black version of *The Wizard of Oz*, you do not hold an audition for beautiful teenage black girls who can sing like crazy… you sign up Diana Ross."

Mahogany and *Lady Sings the Blues* played more to Ross' strengths. In the former, about a fame-drunk fashion designer, she spirals through a confection of hairstyles and hats, along with a beguiling wardrobe the singer herself dreamed up for the role. And in *Lady Sings the Blues*, Ross is totally believable—first as the young Billie Holiday with her hair in humble plaits, on up to her later strung-out performances as Lady Day, with clusters of flowers pinned into her upswept curls.

It's now been nearly 50 years since Ross played those parts and almost 60 since the Supremes' debut. Ensconced on the West Coast, Ross still performs, but at a pace that works for her. Perhaps that's because there is little to prove. As a member of the Supremes, she's already in the Rock and Roll Hall of Fame, and named among *Rolling Stone*'s 100 Greatest Artists of All Time. She has a star on Hollywood's Walk of Fame, and continues to be sampled by artists of her children's generation, including Big Sean and Ariana Grande.

"I went to see her at the Hollywood Bowl this past year, where she was swinging from the stage with her big beautiful hair," Brandly says. "She changed into a different wardrobe several times. She's in her 70s now, and I thought that all that would've slowed down. But to be a celebrity on her level, it's a part of the theatrics. And whenever

"If you want to wear 22 inches of curly hair, shave your head or put on two pairs of false eyelashes, you're living the one life that belongs to you."

Tracee Ellis Ross, Diana's actress daughter, has said it was her mother who inspired her to wear her hair big and out.

> *"She changed into a different wardrobe several times. She's in her 70s now, and I thought that all that would've slowed down..."*

you see her performing, there's always going to be that big hair."

Brandly has also caught Ross out and about. "I ran into her a couple of times at the farmers' market in Hollywood," she says. "When she's there shopping she doesn't have all that hair on, just some type of hat and glasses." As a mother of five, with almost as many grandchildren, Ross admits to wading into the unglamorous realm of changing diapers, meting out discipline and making parental judgment calls that render even a superstar unpopular. "I am more a mother than a celebrity," she writes in *Secrets of a Sparrow*.

Taylor, the *Editor in Chic* author, remembers being around when Ross' mom was still alive. Though Ross and her siblings were raised in Detroit, the family is from the South, where the parenting style was strict and protective. Taylor observed this in the star's approach to rearing her own kids: "She has an old-fashioned sensibility, no matter the modern world she walks in," Taylor says. At the first fashion shoot Taylor did with Ross, the diva's young daughters—Rhonda, Tracee and Chudney—were excitedly watching their mom being photographed (sons Evan and Ross were yet to be born). More recently, Taylor photographed Ross with her now-grown-up daughter, Tracee, an Emmy Award-winning actress on the TV series *Black-ish*. "Her kids say, 'Mom, you were hot!'

That really tickles her," Taylor says with a chuckle. "She loves being thought of as a hot mom." But she's also an involved parent, and stopped the conversation several times during one of Taylor's interview sessions with her to call home and check on the boys.

My *Tenderheaded* co-editor Harris admits that even in this day and age, when women of all races use lace-front wigs and/or weaves to give them a polished appearance or a new look, she can still be judgy about "fake" hair—Ross' included. But seeing gentle moments between the diva and her brood has softened Harris' heart. "About a year ago, at one of those awards shows, all her kids and grandkids came on stage, and she looked like the earth mother that she is," Harris declared. She also found herself moved when Ross participated as a coach on a reality TV show, where aspiring singers battle it out. "She was working with the young singers, and she was really nurturing to them," she says.

Taylor, who remembers being hired a couple of times to style Ross, recalls that all the designers wanted to dress her, and would send her their latest couture in the hopes that she might be seen wearing them around town (or around the world), bringing star power to their brand.

"She was made for this," says Taylor. "It's her divine assignment. Other girls had Barbie, we had Miss Ross."

The Supremes provided the soundtrack to a turbulent era: The war in Vietnam, and the civil rights and women's movements in the US.

Photograph: Harry Langdon/Getty Images, Overleaf photograph: The LIFE Picture Collection/Getty Images

HAIR

70070

Photography by *Emma Hartvig* & Styling by *Sébastien Cambos*

Great Lengths

With hair, as with life, it only takes a slight twist to breathe intrigue into the otherwise ordinary.

Previous spread: Veronika wears a dress by Lemaire. Right: She wears a dress and hat by Jacquemus. Overleaf: Veronika wears a dress by Rochas.

Left: Veronika wears a dress by Lemaire and a hat by Maison Traclet. Above: She wears a dress by Lemaire and gloves by La Bagagerie.

Veronika wears a hat by Mademoiselle Chapeaux and a T-shirt by Acne Studios.

THE
NEW

In Canada, brothers Jagmeet and Gurratan Singh are redressing the stereotype of "image-conscious" politicians.

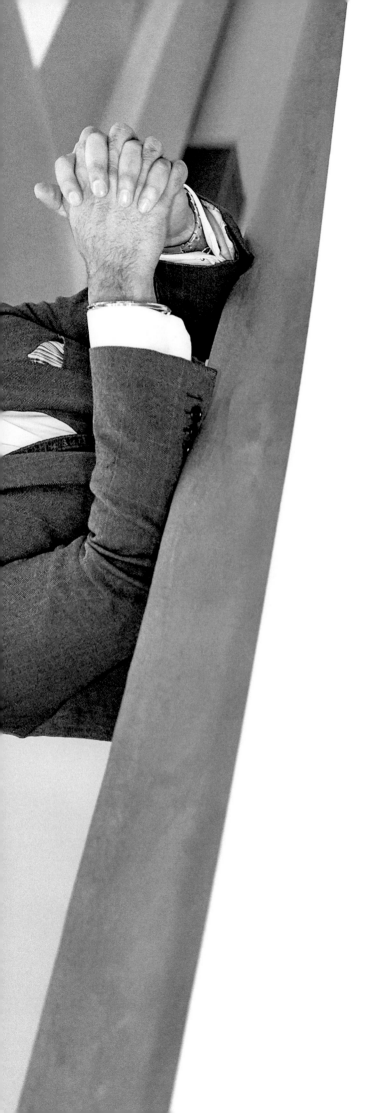

D E M O C R A T S

Words by Chris Frey & Photography by Christopher Ferguson

I t's during a break in our photo shoot at the Toronto Reference Library with Jagmeet Singh, the newly minted leader of Canada's left-wing New Democratic Party, and his brother Gurratan, that it dawns on me—Jagmeet has the job I wanted when I was nine years old.

As a supernerd in the late '70s, I played NDP leader in my school's model parliament, winning our mock election in a landslide. I idolized the party's leader at the time, Ed Broadbent, a former academic from a family of auto workers. This despite the fact that he would never be described as telegenic, dashing or blazingly eloquent—at least not when compared with his rival, Prime Minister Pierre Trudeau, father to current PM, Justin. Rather, Broadbent was often criticized, as his Wikipedia entry notes, "for his long and complex speeches on industrial organization." Such were my interests as a nine-year-old.

On the surface, the contrast between Broadbent and Singh couldn't be sharper. Broadbent, who bore some physical resemblance to Richard Nixon, albeit with a much friendlier face, was a product of the 20th-century labour movement and its aversion to flashiness. Though remembered as a likable campaigner in person, I doubt Broadbent would have had much time for Twitter, Instagram or Snapchat, were such platforms available to him. The 39-year-old Singh, a former litigation lawyer and practicing Sikh, is brawny and movie-star handsome, a tireless preacher of positivity and a popular Instagram dandy. Being born in 1979 may put him at the tail end of Generation X, but in every other way he presents as millennial. Things are often "Awesome!" with Singh.

That he is the first person of color to lead one of Canada's major parties is historic—as are his age and his skill in using social media as a tool for political communications. Even before he had declared his candidacy for the leadership, GQ—a magazine not known for paying much attention to Canadian politicians—interviewed Singh at length, remarking he "understands that the real power of social media isn't showing off his custom-designed suits (though those look sharp as hell), but as a vital tool for communicating with his constituents—the youth, in particular."

With the library's curvy five-story atrium as a backdrop, Singh is photographed wearing a bespoke three-piece navy-blue suit from Toronto's The Dirty Inc., and an olive-green *dastaar*, or turban—a more subdued color choice than the bright pinks and yellows he is often seen in (to provide "pop," he says). An embroidered strap known as a *gatra* is slung across his waistcoat, outlining his muscular frame. "Jagmeet has more of a wrestler's body, with a longer torso," assesses Gurratan, who is standing off to the side. "I have more of a dancer's body—longer legs." Gurratan, 34, serves as his brother's closest advisor and confidant, though when he arrived for the photo shoot he introduced himself as the "stunt double." Behind us a crowd of a dozen people has gathered, mostly young, eager but polite, awaiting the right moment to approach the NDP leader.

It's been the case all day as we make our way about the library: Strangers stopping Singh to take selfies and express their support or admiration, some of whom he greets in their mother tongues. "*Merhaba*," I hear him say to a man identifying himself as Turkic-Afghan. Singh, who is fluent in English, French and Punjabi, claims he is able to greet people in over 40 languages. Agreeing to a photo with one young couple, Singh arches his eyebrows and flashes a sideways peace sign across his beard. The hand sign, known as "chucking a deuce" in hip-hop culture, is one of Singh's go-to selfie poses, though sometimes he will pantomime a theatrical mustache twirl. Throughout all the glad-handing, his enthusiasm never wanes. "One thing I'm really proud of is my energy," Singh tells me later. "I'll want to go to the gym even after a full day of this. This one [assistant], he's 10 years younger than me, he'd ask, after a busy day, 'Aren't you destroyed?' No, I gotta work out!"

Gurratan Singh (left) recently told Canadian newspaper *The Star* that he is considering following his brother Jagmeet (right) into politics.

HAIR

The Toronto Reference Library is as broadly representative a place as you'll find of the city's population—more than half of which was born outside of Canada. Impressive enough is how effortlessly genuine and engaged Singh seems when meeting new people. Even more so is the power of what Singh represents, as evidenced, especially today, by the measure of ardency with which young people of myriad backgrounds buzz around him. He is relatable in a way that few Canadian politicians have ever been, especially among those who have rarely seen much in a politician they could *relate to*.

The comparison to Justin Trudeau is unavoidable: Singh comes across as an at-ease street-level campaigner, who might actually enjoy all the town halls and meet-and-greets, whereas Trudeau can seem like he's trying much too hard to get everyone to *like* him. (Efforts to appear "woke" are a related complaint.) A recent profile in *Toronto Life* magazine not unfairly described Singh as "the left's greatest showman," the tone dialed as a compliment.

II

His swift rise to political stardom already has pundits asking whether Singh has the potential to be Trudeau's "worst nightmare"—a bold conjecture considering that Singh leads a party that has never won power nationally, and does not himself currently hold a seat in the federal parliament.

Historically, Trudeau's center-left Liberal Party has appropriated NDP policies whenever it seemed politically viable. Many of the social programs Canadians prize most, such as universal health care, originated with the NDP, but the Liberals take the credit. In the last election, Trudeau actually won by running *to the left* of the NDP on many economic issues, including deficit spending. Now, with signs that the electorate is trending leftward, the hope is that not only will Singh return the party to its roots—but that he might even provide the winning model for 21st-century progressive politics. The signature issues in which Singh has planted his party's flag neatly reflect the zeitgeist: the increasingly precarious nature of work, immigrant rights, income inequality and the environment. As the journalist Michael Harris put it, "Singh is the ideal political leader to make the case that millennials deserve a better shake [...] and that he is the real progressive in the conversation."

And a politician couldn't ask for a more appealing up-by-the-bootstraps origin story. Jagtaran Singh, Jagmeet's father, arrived in Toronto from India's Punjab state and endured a fate typical for many educated immigrants to Canada—not having his professional credentials recognized in his new home. Already a family physician in India, Jagtaran worked several jobs, including as a security guard, in order to again put himself through medical school and then train as a psychiatrist. He and his wife, Harmeet Kaur, a teacher also originally from Punjab, raised three children—Jagmeet, Gurratan and daughter Manjot—mostly in Windsor, an industrial town in southwestern Ontario where Jagtaran worked as head of psychiatry at a hospital and later started his own private practice. As a child, Jagmeet suffered such racist abuse from classmates that his parents switched him to a prep school across the border in Detroit. At 21, while Jagmeet was in London, Ontario, pursuing his undergraduate studies in biology, his father became sick and unable to work. Gurratan, then 16, was sent to live with his older brother.

"When I moved in with Jagmeet, he suddenly had a high schooler to feed and sustain," Gurratan tells me later in the evening, over dinner at Planta, a vegetarian restaurant in Toronto's Yorkville neighborhood. (The brothers are vegetarian and abstain from alcohol.) All at once, Jagmeet was a student, family breadwinner and surrogate father. It was during this time, Gurratan says, that Jagmeet "opened my eyes to a lot of social justice issues and looking at the world through a different lens." There was an obvious synergy whenever they discussed politics, and Gurratan, who would follow in his brother's footsteps and attend law school, recognized in his older brother a born leader. "He already had this natural charisma," he says.

And yet Jagmeet insists he was a reluctant politician. The idea to run as an NDP candidate in the federal election of May 2011 came from Gurratan and a group of close friends, all of whom were active in social justice issues locally. "[Jagmeet] was always giving guidance and direction to the work we were doing, mentoring us," says Gurratan. "It just came to a point where we saw a lack of people in our community advocating, representing the issues we cared about, like refugee and immigrant rights, poverty, social justice. We thought we needed to put someone forward who could be that voice."

Though Jagmeet says he was, at the time, "satisfied where I was as a lawyer" which included a share of pro bono work and advocating for refugee and immigrant rights, Gurratan was relentless. While one friend, Amneet Singh Bali, Jagmeet's future campaign manager during his leadership run, complimented him on his natural leadership qualities, his brother played the bad cop. "He would tell me, 'You can't pass up this chance to help the community—you're going to let everybody down,'" remembers Jagmeet. "There was a lot of guilt tripping." It took six months to convince Jagmeet to run.

"As a brown-skinned bearded man, I don't have the luxury of not worrying about how I look. There are a lot of negative stereotypes and prejudices that I've had to dispel or disarm."

According to a 2017 poll, three in 10 Canadian voters said they "could not vote" for a turban-wearing Sikh man.

Stylist: Amber Watkins

HAIR

That first election day, Jagmeet surprised everyone when he came within 500 votes of beating the race's incumbent. Still, he figured that was the end of it. But when a provincial election was called a few months later Jagmeet was again encouraged to run. This time it was more than just a group of friends. "I got hundreds and hundreds of calls, people saying they want me to run again, [and] 'We didn't realize you would come so close.' It made me think now is the time, I don't see myself doing this again in the future." Only six months after his first try, Jagmeet won, eventually rising to become deputy leader of the opposition NDP in the provincial legislature.

Though Gurratan may have been the one who pushed him into politics, Jagmeet's values were passed down from earlier generations. His great-grandfather, Sewa Singh Thikriwala, was a Punjabi martyr and folk hero who led uprisings against colonialism in the early 20th century. He died of starvation from a hunger strike while in prison. More essential was his mother, who instilled in Jagmeet the spiritual values of Sikhism, though his father was non-observant. "On a fundamental level, [Sikhism says] the universe may be diverse, with different life forms and types of people, from different places speaking different languages—but we all have a common thread that connects us. We are all one."

It's from this starting point, Jagmeet says, that Sikh philosophy asserts a moral obligation to defend the rights of others—hence his passion for social justice. "This is why we wear the kirpan," he explains, referring to the curved ceremonial knife Sikh men are required to wear. "Kirpan literally means *grace* and *honor*. The oath that we take with grace and honor is to defend the rights of all people, and that we can't be passive when we see injustice happening around us."

"We can't be passive when we see injustice happening around us."

Growing up as part of a racial minority, however, defending others first meant learning how to defend himself. At eight years old, while living in Windsor, Jagmeet began growing his hair out according to the Sikh practice known as *kes*, and wearing a turban. The bullying got instantly worse, prompting Jagmeet to sign up for aikido and taekwondo; by high school, he was captain of the wrestling team. (These days, he still trains in Brazilian jujitsu.)

Whatever antagonism Jagmeet encountered only reaffirmed his sense of who he was, both as an individual and as part of a larger community. "The whole point of kes in Sikhism is an acceptance of our natural way of being, accepting yourself in a deeper way," he says. "If there's gray hair coming in or it's frizzy I don't worry about it. There's something relaxing and beautiful about that." It's symbolic, he adds, of the necessity to make peace with oneself. "When I see more gray coming in, it's a reminder that we're mortal," says Gurratan. "That we have limited time on this earth and [we need] to make the most of it. What we wear is an expression of the values we aspire to." In the case of growing up Sikh in North America, he adds, "there's this incredibly strong social aspect to it—we can't hide who we are or where we're from."

And their religion is something Gurratan and Jagmeet see no reason to downplay, or claim as a private matter, anyway—rather they are happy to talk about it whenever asked. Not just to demystify it, but to show how well its values accord with a progressive view of the country, and perhaps where the culture is moving more generally. "This whole [movement] we're seeing today toward well-being is what Sikh spirituality is all about," says Gurratan, noting that popular mindfulness practices such as meditation and fasting are core to Sikhism. "Sikhism is about connectedness—with other people and your own inner light."

III

When Jagmeet announced his NDP leadership bid in May 2017, he was by far the least known nationally among the four main contenders. During his time in the Ontario provincial legislature, he had done little to distinguish himself, with the notable exception of introducing a motion to prohibit the controversial police practice of "carding"—random ID checks that, studies have shown, disproportionately target young men of color. The issue was a personal one for Singh, who estimates he has been spot-checked about 10 times. "Whenever I was stopped by police," he says, "it made me feel like something was wrong with me. It erases the value of all your hard work in life, like you don't have meaning." Singh's motion passed the house unanimously.

Beyond that, he had made a splash more for his bespoke suits and the bon vivant lifestyle he documented over social media. Then, with just three weeks to go in the leadership campaign, came the viral moment that mattered. During a rally at a recreation center in the Toronto suburb of Brampton, a woman named Jennifer Bush got up in Singh's face, shouting accusations that he supported the Muslim Brotherhood and sharia law. Rather than correcting her by explaining that he was Sikh and not Muslim, Singh retained his composure. "We don't want to be intimidated by hate," Singh said to the crowd, before turning to Bush. "We welcome you, we love you, we all believe in your rights."

When a video of the incident was posted to YouTube, it became an instant global sensation, racking up more than 50 million views and praise for Singh's cool handling of the situation. By the eve of the leadership vote, Singh had raised more money and signed up more new party members than any of his rivals. With 53 percent of the vote, he won in the first round of balloting.

Later, Singh would admit to *Maclean's* magazine that, "in a way, my whole life prepared me for this [incident]. I've faced much more aggressive situations where I had to defend myself." From an early age, he understood that if he carried himself in a certain way it would "reduce the amount of people who would want to fight with me," he now says. And if people were going to stare at him, Singh decided he would give them something to look at. As a teen that meant baggy jeans and a hip-hop aesthetic. It wasn't until Singh graduated law school that he acquired the taste for elegant, English-cut suits that he's known for today. While other articling students bought as many suits at discount stores as their budget would allow, Singh treated clothes as an investment, buying fewer but higher-quality pieces and rotating them through an entire year. "I don't think they ever realized I only had two suits," he says, crediting the impression he made with helping him attract a healthy roster of new clients.

Not surprisingly, Singh's easygoing fashionableness has elicited some skepticism about his seriousness as a politician. Though he has been successful at keying in on his core issues, he is at his weakest when articulating policy, both in the small details and the big vision. Questions of style and image over substance already bedevil Justin Trudeau, as he heads into the last year of his mandate. When I ask Singh whether his own posh image might detract from both his message and accomplishments, he turns the question, and its assumptions, inside out. "As a brown-skinned bearded man, I don't have the luxury of not worrying about how I look," he says. "There are a lot of negative stereotypes and prejudices that I've had to dispel or disarm, and I did that through the way I dressed. My clothing is like social armor."

Singh has spoken of his style in this way before, but that hasn't stopped critics from framing next year's campaign as "Justin versus Jagmeet in the GQ election." Singh need only look to the man he hopes to unseat as prime minister for a cautionary tale—that the seeming obsession with image and wokeness will only get him so far, until one day, very quickly, it becomes a liability. Exhibit A: Trudeau's diplomatic trip to India in February, during which he was ruthlessly mocked for going way over the top with traditional Indian outfits.

In interviews, Singh talks a lot about authenticity. On social media he promotes *The Authenticity Principle* by his friend Ritu Bhasin—a leadership book that argues "choosing to live authentically is the most important step you can take to thrive in your personal life, your relationships and your career." Bhasin's thesis has special resonance with members of racial minorities who feel constantly pressured to conform within mainstream society. But there is also the risk, particularly acute for a politician, of being so consciously "authentic" as to read as inauthentic.

IV

So far, Donald Trump's right-wing populism hasn't gained much traction north of the border. But that doesn't mean Singh's ascendance isn't, at least in part, a manifestation of the same disruptions occurring to the political process, mainly via technology, but also through popular culture—even if he clearly comes from the opposite end of the political spectrum from Trump. Editorial writers who express discomfort with Singh's media savviness, snappy looks and upbeat message are perhaps missing the point.

A couple of weeks after my interview with Singh, during a livestreamed interview, the NDP leader was asked by the journalist Paul Wells to assess the country's mood, given that unemployment is near an all-time low. "People feel okay about the government," Singh allowed, "but they feel stuck in their lives." Singh framed the problem in terms of economic inequality, a disproportionate share of the gains in income going to the already wealthy. Singh added that "I think [Trudeau] means well, but there's a dissonance, where for him it's maybe an academic discussion when he talks about fairness or inequality." Singh then pivoted to his own struggles, of knowing precariousness and bigotry firsthand. In recent speeches, Singh seems to be test-driving a phrase that could serve as his slogan in the next election: "This is not as good as it gets."

Gurratan understands the seismic shift that his brother represents, not just in politics, but in Canadian society in its broadest sense, and what it means to belong. "For the children of immigrants, and young people of color across the board," he says, "we're supposed to feel Canadian, but there's a sense sometimes that you don't experience it. For the people who focus on [Jagmeet's] style over substance, there's this whole other conversation to be had that Jagmeet represents what all parents, and particularly immigrant parents, want for their children: That they can come to a new country and their child actually has a chance to be prime minister."

"If there's gray hair coming in or it's frizzy, I don't worry about it."

NAÏM ABBOUD
A BRUSH WITH HISTORY

TEXT: CAROLE CORM

Beirut, 1957. Naïm Abboud takes a job in the hair salon of the Saint Georges—the most storied hotel in the Middle East. As his career progresses, the princesses, pop stars and exiled politicians of the region all flock to him for his va-va-voom take on haute coiffure. In her biography of Abboud, who is now in his 70s and runs a salon in London, Carole Corm traces not only the glamorous, golden trajectory of the Middle East's most sought-after hairdresser, but the political turmoil of the region that he witnessed firsthand.

Tante Alice's day began with a visit from her hairdresser. Each day, while sitting at her art deco dressing table, she would have her hair done up in a netted bun. Her hairdresser, Clovis, would go to Tante Alice's sprawling, antique-filled flat before setting off to work at Beirut's Saint Georges Hotel, which had a popular hair salon. Clovis had an imposing character, a long face and stern expression, not to mention one of those historical names that the Christian Lebanese, in deference to the French mandate forces, gave to their children in the first half of the 20th century. (Other popular names included Charles de Gaulle and Jeanne d'Arc.)

Before Naïm Abboud left for work, he would often sit and watch Clovis do his aunt's hair. One morning, Clovis suggested the teenager come and work with him at the Saint Georges. Naïm had grown uneasy with his colleagues at the salon where he was currently working. The staff there were mostly older hairdressers who flirted with him unabashedly. Still very young and uncomfortable with anything that had to do with sex—all the more so since his only experience had been violent and brutal—he seized the offer to work at the Saint Georges as the perfect way out.

Then the Middle East's most iconic hotel, the Saint Georges was the place to see and be seen. Political coups were set in motion there, oil deals negotiated and strategic alliances formed. As the journalist Said K. Aburish wrote in *Beirut Spy*, his book about the Saint Georges'

bar and the political dealings that took place there, "Beirut was the center of the Middle East, so the undisputed center of Beirut was the Saint Georges Hotel." The Saint Georges was made all the more inviting, writes Aburish, by the fact that "almost every participant in the affairs of the hotel, right down to the most humble employee, was moved by something beyond mere duty."

Madame Boueiri, an astute Lebanese woman who kept a room at the hotel throughout the year, owned the Saint Georges' hair salon. She found Naïm's French and good manners impressive and adopted him instantly. At first, as in his previous job and owing to his young age, he wasn't allowed to style women's hair; he had to watch and learn from more senior hairdressers. By watching others, however, he realized that some clients weren't getting the best results. One day he mustered up the courage to ask May Moussa, a regular at the salon, if she would let him style her hair just this once. The wife of the director of the Casino du Liban liked to help young people, especially if they had talent, and she agreed.

At that time, many Lebanese women wanted to look like the French actress Brigitte Bardot, who had been introduced to the world in the 1957 film *And God Created Woman*. Naïm gave Moussa the Bardot look, and from then on, his career took off. Moussa wasn't just any client. At the casino, Moussa hosted European royalty, US presidents and many singers who gave

concerts in its Las Vegas–style playhouse. Until 1964, the casino also served as the setting for the Miss Europe beauty pageant (with famous French hairdressers flown in for the occasion).

Moussa told her high society friends about Naïm and they came knocking. As she was often photographed in magazines, even more women would come to the salon asking for the young prodigy. "Despite being shy, we all felt he would go far," says a long-time client. The "Brigitte Bardot of the Orient," as Moussa was sometimes called, would open other doors for Naïm as well: She offered him styling jobs with Dior models and the Miss Europe beauty contestants.

Because the Saint Georges was also the hotel of choice for anyone passing through Beirut, a variety of celebrities came into the salon. Nahla Abdel Wahab, the wife of musician Mohamed Abdel Wahab, who composed many songs for the Egyptian diva Umm Kulthum, became a loyal client. There were actresses too. Jayne Mansfield, who had opted to stay at the newly opened Phoenicia Hotel, still came to the Saint Georges to get her hair done. And Anita Ekberg, Federico Fellini's femme fatale in *La Dolce Vita*, was coiffed by Naïm before setting out for dinner at the fashionable Le Chandelier.

Not only celebrities came to the Saint Georges, however. Cosmopolitan and liberated Beirut proved a magnet for exiled politicians and their wives as they fled authoritarian regimes back home. Narriman [Sadek], whose former husband King Farouk of Egypt had been deposed by [Gamal Abdel] Nasser in 1952, had since remarried and began to spend a lot of time in Lebanon. She kept a room at the Saint Georges and visited Naïm regularly. He even created special bangs for the former queen that curled in front of the ear and which he poetically called *la mèche amoureuse* (the enamored hair bang).

Another famous exile at the hotel was the Iraqi singer Affifa Iskandar, sometimes known as "The Umm Kulthum of Iraq," who had been close to the royal court of the young King Faisal II of Iraq before he and his relatives were brutally murdered in the 1958 coup. Iskandar's popularity was such, however, that the fierce Abd al-Karim Qasim, the Iraqi dictator who had replaced the monarchy, sent emissaries to the Saint Georges to plead with her to return. According to Aburish in *Beirut Spy*, she held an "exalted position among her compatriots" from the Saint Georges Hotel. Naïm, however, remembers a sad lady, "who used to cry all the time."

The Saint Georges hair salon became so popular that the manager, Jean Bertolet, had to put chairs in the corridors to keep people comfortable while waiting. India Abdini, May Moussa's sister, remembers Naïm in those days. "He combined two characteristics that don't usually go together," she says. "He had a steely determination yet managed to be extremely kind."

Around that time, Moussa, showing once again that she had her protégé's interests at heart, offered Naïm a trip to Paris to learn from the great French hairdressers. The local press wrote about the journey and joked that he had packed *labneh* (Lebanese strained yogurt) and olives in his suitcase. He hadn't, but the article

made plain that he'd gained a reputation, albeit with a whiff of condescension—he was still very young, only 17 at that time. In Paris, Naïm stayed in a hotel on rue Pasquier, near the Madeleine church. On one occasion an Algerian man helped him find his way back to the hotel. When they entered the lobby together, the receptionist hurled insults at the Algerian, betraying an unabashed racist streak that shocked Naïm, who knew little of the troubles France then faced across the Mediterranean.

In the late '50s, along with Alexandre de Paris, sisters Maria and Rosy Carita dominated Parisian haute coiffure with their beautiful chignons. Despite an introduction by the Lebanese beauty May Arida ("No one can do your hair like Naïm, and he is so quick—*oh là là*"), the two were rather cold when Naïm called on them. He toured their salon and that was it. On the other hand, he barely needed Moussa's introduction to meet Claude Maxime. The bubbly lady who'd started off her career with Jacques Dessange and styled Brigitte Bardot herself welcomed the teenager warmly and told him where he could buy hair accessories in Paris. In the next few years, at Moussa's invitation, Maxime would travel several times to Lebanon to style the Miss Europe beauty pageant taking place at the casino. There, she would meet Naïm again and the two became good friends.

Since opening in 1959, the casino had become a popular concert hall for visiting singers and performers. In January 1963, the day before his concert, the so-called French Elvis, Johnny Hallyday, was banned from performing by the conservative politician Kamal Jumblatt. (Jumblatt had also tried, unsuccessfully, to stop the Twist from spreading to Lebanon's nightclubs.) Moussa consoled Hallyday by giving him a silver handgun and touring him around

the country. The French rocker visited Byblos, dined at the casino's nightclub, the Baccarat, and even managed a stop at the Saint Georges for a haircut by Naïm. The next day, the Lebanese daily *L'Orient* reported how a dozen hysterical fans had descended on the salon clamoring for a lock of Johnny's blond hair.

Women didn't just want a piece of the visiting rock star, however, they also wanted Naïm. "Naïm is a real artist. He would put hairpieces, pearls and ribbons in our hair. We looked like Christmas trees, but very chic Christmas trees," says Liliane Fattal-Arida. Mrs. Parker, a rich American woman, thought the world of the Lebanese hairdresser. She suggested Naïm move to New York. Her proposal received backing a few weeks later in a letter penned by Eva Curtis, manager of the Les Elles salon on Madison Avenue. Ms. Curtis offered him a job at $120 a week. It was a tempting offer, but he lacked the confidence; he couldn't speak English and, anyway, too much was happening in Beirut for him to seriously contemplate leaving everything behind.

Now wealthy enough to lead the life he pleased, the young man decided it was time to move out from Tante Alice's flat. He must have been about 19 when he rented a furnished apartment amongst the modernist buildings and trendy cafés in the neighborhood of Hamra. It was just a stepping stone for the penthouse he would soon come to rent in the bourgeois neighborhood of Badaro, not too far from where he grew up. He also bought himself a black Jaguar (in monthly installments) and started a collection of oriental antiques, perhaps as a way to recreate the environment he had seen and liked in his grandmother's and aunt's houses. Sarkis, the Armenian antique dealer at the Saint Georges, whom he saw

"A few months later, four armed robbers attacked the salon. Revolvers in hand, they threatened the terrified clients. Sabah, the late Lebanese pop star, who was at the salon that day, hid in the toilets."

every day on his way to work, advised Naïm on his first purchases of opaline glass flasks and lamps.

As Naïm's career bloomed, the young man stumbled on a small article reporting the murder of the man who had sexually abused him in his youth. It was a shocking discovery and one that put a definitive end to a sad chapter of his childhood and adolescence.

In 1975, Naïm told the press that honey blond was out. It was all about auburn. "The girl to follow is Georgina Rizk," he explained, referring to the Lebanese beauty queen who had been elected Miss Universe four years earlier. The attractive redhead regularly posed in the Lebanese press with Naïm's hairstyle creations. Her incredible rise to fame, and her later marriage to a Palestine Liberation Organization fighter, seemed to be a kind of metaphor for the country itself. Despite its international reputation for cosmopolitan glamour, Lebanon had fallen under the spell of a dangerous liaison.

In 1969, the Palestinian fighters who had been expelled from Jordan converged on Lebanon. Here, under the terms of the Cairo Agreement, they could regroup in the decrepit refugee camps and arm themselves. In effect, Lebanon was turning into a launch pad from which to fight Israel. The Palestinian cause divided the nation. While many Lebanese people supported the struggle, others vehemently opposed it as a violation of Lebanon's sovereignty. The divisions mostly fell along religious lines, and the tension grew to an explosive pitch. An influential Saudi princess warned Naïm that it was time to "forget Lebanon."

Like most of his compatriots, he didn't take the warnings seriously. He directly witnessed more warning signs than the average Lebanese

person, but he still wanted to believe that everything would turn out all right. En route to Kuwait, where he'd been hired to style a wedding, he remembered seeing a curious-looking man wearing a wig; questioned by airport security, the man said he worked for the Red Crescent. But when Naïm saw him again on the plane, the man had a Kalashnikov slung over his shoulder. "He and his friends told us the plane was filled with bombs. We landed in Kuwait and after a few long hours, they freed the women and children." Naïm tried to sneak out with them, but they stopped him.

"Everyone on the plane knew who I was, including the hostage takers. I was in a complete panic, I felt I was about to have a heart attack." At 6 a.m. the following day, the hijackers took pity on him and told him he could leave. Convinced they would shoot him in the back, Naïm refused to exit the aircraft. Luckily, negotiations had taken place and the rest of the passengers were soon freed. May Arida, whose husband was in the airline business, helped him return to Lebanon. He wasn't the only one who came back. Five days later, the hijackers stopped by the salon asking for money. "I didn't have any, so I offered to take care of their girlfriends' and sisters' hair."

A few months later, four armed robbers attacked the salon. Revolvers in hand, they threatened the terrified clients. Sabah [the late Lebanese pop star], who was at the salon that day, hid in the toilets. Another client, Racil Chalhoub, who had been going to Naïm's since she was 15, found refuge in the small room where towels were being washed. To escape the robbers' attention, she threw her jewelry in the used coffee cups next to the sink. Naïm was less fortunate. He handed over all his chains and the Boucheron watch inscribed with his

name, which the Kuwaiti princess and poet Souad Moubarak al Sabah had given him. The other clients obliged as well. Two days later the police traced the stolen jewelry and the robbers back to the neighborhood of Hamra. They were working for one of the myriad political factions operating in Lebanon at the time.

Following the incident, several competing militias in the country offered to post bodyguards at the entrance of the salon. Naïm refused, declaring that his salon was no cabaret. When war officially broke out in 1975, Naïm was in the thick of it. He was passing through the neighborhood of Furn al Shebak on his way back from Damascus, where he had been shopping for antiques, when an attack on Christian leader Pierre Gemayel led to a violent retaliation against Palestinians traveling in a bus nearby. The attack on the bus marked the beginning of the long and complicated Lebanese civil war. It would last 15 years. The hotel neighborhood was Beirut's first to ignite as Christian militias battled pro-Palestinian forces in what quickly became known as "the Battle of the Hotels." The salon, which was just up the hill, was ransacked.

Naïm heard stories of clients' hairpieces being sold on the streets. And that wasn't all. He couldn't get to his house located in Badaro, close to the military hospital and the dangerous Green Line, which now severed Beirut into Christian and Muslim zones. Naïm soon heard that the building's guard, an affable Sudanese man, had been shot trying to protect it. "I realized then that life wasn't only about scissors and hairpins."

—

This article is an abridged and edited excerpt from Naïm: A Brush with History (Darya Press, 2013).

At Work With:
Sherin Khankan

In 2015, *Sherin Khankan* led the first Friday prayer at Copenhagen's all-women Mariam Mosque. Three years down the line, she talks to *Alia Gilbert* about finding feminist role models in scripture, spiritual self-care and the importance of swimming twice a day. Photography by *Hördur Ingason*.

HAIR

Styling: Kenneth Pihl Nissen, Hair and Makeup: Line Bille

When Sherin Khankan established the first female-led mosque in Scandinavia, she was celebrated in the mainstream press for being a feminist activist in addition to being its imam. Khankan, however, makes it refreshingly clear that the two roles are one and the same. An Islamic scholar, she is an expert on the ancient primary source texts that swat away today's patriarchal interpretations of institutional Islamic thought. "At the time of the Prophet, women were warriors. They were teachers. And, of course, they were imams," she says. Khankan is a steadfast community activist (she founded Exitcirclen, an organization for psychologically abused women), humble in her roots ("My father's homemade shawarma is the only shawarma I like") and a lifelong academic. In August, she will qualify as a cognitive psychotherapist, a role that she will combine with her existing work as a spiritual leader and imam at Mariam Mosque. On top of this, Khankan is a mother of four. She is an exceptionally difficult woman to pin down.

When did the idea of a women-run, women-focused mosque come to you? It has been a long journey—it wasn't just an idea that we had overnight. It began back in 1999 when I was doing my thesis on Sufism and Islamic activism in Damascus at the Abu al-Nur Mosque. I spent eight months there doing my fieldwork. I first thought about female imams and muftis [scholars] while studying the history of female leadership in Islam. The vision for Mariam Mosque began there.

The "Mariam" in Mariam Mosque refers to the Virgin Mary. Why did you choose to name the mosque after her? The Virgin Mary is a unifying figure, which is what the Mariam Mosque is all about. It's about unifying the manipulated dichotomies we've created in this world—dichotomies between East and West, Christian and Muslim, women and men, black and white, homosexuals and heterosexuals, faithful practicing Muslims and secularists. The Virgin Mary has a *surah* [chapter] named after her in the Quran, and some Islamic scholars believe that she was a prophet. She is one of many female role models in the Islamic tradition. I also see Mariam as a metaphor for the concept of birth and rebirth. All chapters in the Quran start with "In the name of God, the most gracious, the most merciful." In Arabic, the words for

"gracious" and "merciful" come from the word that refers to the womb. God is merciful and shows mercy—like the womb, which contains life and gives life. This was also one of the things that I thought about when choosing the name.

Were there naysayers? Many people told us that it would be impossible and that it wasn't necessary. Many said that it would create too much chaos. It did not. Mariam Mosque has really given me hope because now we have an international voice. I view this as a huge responsibility, not only to challenge the patriarchal structures within the religious institution but also the growing anti-Islamic rhetoric and propaganda.

Was the fact of the mosque being women-only always a given? I actually voted against having the mosque exclusively for women for Friday prayer. I wanted to have it mixed, but the board voted me down. And today, I feel very happy about that. It was a wise decision. I realized that when you want to create change, you have to do it very carefully while understanding the community you are a part of. With Mariam Mosque being a women's mosque, we are on safe ground. Women love this space because it's sacred, only for them.

What did you see that changed your mind? Magical things happen when you are in a room that's exclusively for women. Women dare to go further. We've talked about issues and taboos that we would never have talked about if there were men in the space. Many women seek Islamic spiritual care for very sensitive issues, and the fact that it's a women's mosque on Fridays makes it possible for us to serve them in a better way. Ultimately, being an imam is about servitude.

The history of female Islamic leaders isn't something that gets brought up very often. Can you tell me more about it? Female imams are not a new phenomenon. Many people—and many Muslims—don't know that. The idea of female imams isn't a recent revolution. It actually goes back to Islamic roots, to the time of the Prophet. We've had female imams in China since the 1820s. There are female imams in Somalia, South Africa, Germany, Canada and the United States. These are the stories we have to tell—the stories that are left untold.

Did you always plan on becoming one of the imams at the mosque? Actually, in the beginning, I only wanted to recruit female imams and be the woman behind the mosque. But slowly, I grew into the role. I had a lot of experience in Islamic spiritual care—I had taken a course at Copenhagen University in 2014. I started with the Islamic spiritual care, then Islamic marriages and then eventually I just started doing all of the things that imams do. Finally, I took the title upon me. Saliha Marie Fetteh was one of the other recruited imams at the mosque, and together we led the first Friday prayer when it opened in 2015.

The mosque was 15 years in the making. What was leading that first Friday prayer like for you? It was really amazing. There were 70 women in the room—40 Muslims and 30 non-Muslims. It was so beautiful having the non-Muslims praying together with us. When they went down in *sujood* [kneeling in prayer] with us, it was truly a metaphor for the unifying force that the mosque was based on.

I'd like to touch on this issue's theme. Hair has become a divisive topic when it comes to mainstream dialogue on Muslims and Islamophobia. Well, I'd like to say that I respect any woman's right to wear the scarf or not to wear the scarf, to cover the hair or not to cover the hair. It's an integral part of the [U.N.'s Universal] Declaration of Human Rights. It's stated very clearly that anyone has the right to practice his or her religion in the private and public sphere. When the scarf is denounced and the center of discussion, I think it's very problematic because you're actually denying a woman a basic human right—the right to choose. But of course, if women are forced to wear the scarf, I fight for their right not to wear it. In Mariam Mosque, I have young women coming to me to talk about whether to wear the hijab or to take it off. We have female spiritual leaders who wear the scarf and those who do not. We leave the choice up to them, and I think that's very important. There's that fairy tale about the woman with long hair, I don't know if you know it? She's locked in a tower.

Yes, I think it's the story of Rapunzel. I had many thoughts about it when I was little. She's trapped, and locked up in a tower. She's not allowed to go outside, and a person climbs into the tower using her hair. I think the story could be used as a metaphor both for empowerment but also restraint. And someone cuts her hair in the end, right?

Khankan grew up in a household that combined two different cultures. Her father is a Muslim refugee from Syria, her mother is Christian and from Finland.

"*I respect any woman's right to cover the hair or not to cover the hair.*"

"I'm very good at taking care of my own needs. I know what I like."

Khankan sees her training in cognitive psychotherapy as a natural extension of her duty of care as an imam.

"In the beginning, you always think it's impossible to change the status quo."

I think it was a witch that cut her hair to prevent her from seeing anyone from the outside world again. I'll have to read it again. There are also stories of women who do not want to cut their hair, ever, because they feel that they become an adult, somehow. There are different metaphors you could use. It's interesting—I've had many discussions about the scarf, but not about hair. I love hair. I love long hair. I've always had long hair. I think I cut my hair once when I was very young, but since then, it has always been long.

You've mentioned a few times that Mariam Mosque offers Islamic spiritual care. This is the first time I've learned about this concept in Islam. Is it a practice related to self-care? They are the same thing—Islamic spiritual care is self-care. The Prophet said that you have to know yourself in order to know others. And in order to help others, you must help yourself first. Islamic spiritual care is about meeting people on their own terms, without judgments, without valuations. It's about guidance. There's a beautiful poem by Rumi, the Sufi poet, called "The Guest House." Do you know it?

Yes, I love that poem. It compares the human experience to a guesthouse, meaning that all "guests"—like difficult emotions, experiences and so on—should be welcomed with open arms. It's very comforting. Yes, it is. "The Guest House" is the essence of Islamic spiritual care. It's about acceptance. It's like [Reinhold Niebuhr's] "Serenity Prayer"—about finding the strength to accept the things you cannot change, the courage to change the things that you can and the wisdom to know the difference. We don't get to decide our families or where we're born. There are some conditions that are very difficult. We have a lot of people coming to Mariam Mosque that have very deep wounds because of things that have happened in their family. All their lives, they have been repeating unhealthy patterns or else trying to fight bad patterns.

How do you help them? In some cases, we use stories from the Quran or from Islamic tradition. But Islamic spiritual care can be totally different in other cases. It depends on the person. Sometimes, the stories don't comfort the woman in front of me. The comfort comes from somewhere else. Cognitive psychotherapy can be more useful in these instances. This summer, I'll finish my studies in cognitive psychotherapy. I mix cognitive psychotherapy with Islamic spiritual care, and it has become very successful as more and more people hear about it.

How do you take care of yourself? I've recently realized that I'm very good at taking care of my own needs. I know what I like—and my self-care is swimming in the ocean. I swim in the ocean all year-round, except for two months [in winter] when it's very difficult for me. I need it. It's what keeps me alive and somehow it gives me strength, spiritually. In the summertime when it's warm, I swim two or three times a day—one time with the children, and the other times either when it's very late and they are all asleep, or early in the morning before everyone wakes up. But self-care is a tricky question for a mother of four children who are between the ages of six and 13 years old [laughs].

Mashallah **[God bless]!** Yes, so of course I am very focused on their needs. There's a difference between doing things that are meaningful, and doing things that make your soul blossom. I work full time at the Mariam Mosque, and it gives great meaning to my life. But what makes my soul truly blossom is being with my children.

How do you stay organized with everything you have on your plate? Actually, I have a huge calendar, and people laugh when they see it. I carry it with me everywhere. And I always carry pencils with me in 10 different colors. I don't write anything on my phone, and actually very little on the computer. I'm traditional in that sense, and it works very well for me.

Going back to that first Friday prayer you gave at Mariam Mosque, what was it like for your children to see you do that? When I gave the first Friday prayer, all my children were standing beside me while I was preparing. They knew it was a historic day. That something big was happening. Halima, who was five at the time, had one of her friends over who was Danish. She whispered to Halima, "What is happening? Why is your mother dressing like that? What is an imam, anyway?" Halima looked at her with very proud eyes and said loudly, "An imam is a woman who is doing great things." I'll never forget it. It gives me hope. In the beginning, you always think it's impossible to change the status quo. But actually, it is possible.

In many male-dominated mosques, women are encouraged to pray at home or in small auxiliary sections.

Hair may be a thing of beauty, but it can cause trouble when it turns up in the wrong place. Words by *Pip Usher*

HAIR:
On Trial
In Food
Under Hats
All Over

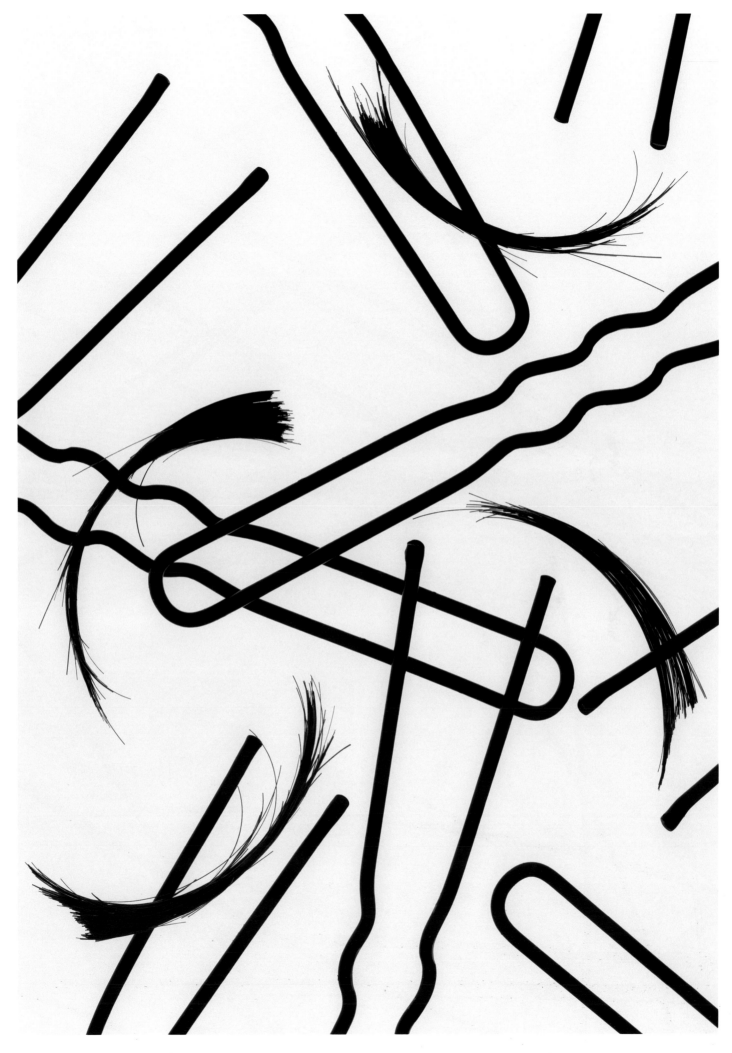

Falling Short

The courtroom's atmosphere is electric as the prosecutor strides to the front. Holding up a transparent bag, she reveals her trump card: a hair from the accused found at the scene of the crime. One look at the jury's faces and it's clear this case is closed. Who can argue with the damning proof of forensic science, right?

Wrong, says Ruth Morgan, professor of crime and forensic sciences at University College London and director of the UCL Centre for Forensic Sciences. While forensic science plays an important role in the reconstruction of a crime, she says, it's dangerous to place undue emphasis upon a strand of hair: "It can be possible to put more weight on a piece of evidence than we've got the data to support."

Forensic science is predicated on the principle that every contact leaves a trace. As we interact with the environment around us, we simultaneously leave materials behind and collect them on our own person. Hair, along with other pieces of evidence, helps investigators piece together a picture of where contact has been made. Examining a sample closely under a microscope, they decipher its history. Did it come from a human or an animal? Does it belong to the victim or someone else? Was it from the head or the body? Did it get ripped from the root or was it naturally shed?

Yet even as a back story emerges from microscopic hair examinations—some of which can present a very persuasive case against a suspect—Morgan insists on the importance of an ongoing and robust interrogation of the forensic evidence. "It's very difficult to prove that a hair is there because of a direct transfer," she says. "An indirect transfer could happen when you sit on a bus and leave a hair on the seat and then another person sits down and picks your hair up on their jacket and that hair can then be transferred on. You had direct contact with a seat, Person B had direct contact with the seat, and then Person B had direct contact with Person C."

In other words, prosecutors' reliance on microscopic hair comparisons to link a defendant to a crime is a bad idea. In recent years, mitochondrial DNA testing has started to take precedence. Found in the hair shaft, mitochondrial DNA can tell us about the hair owner's genetic identification and profiling. Yet even this technology remains riddled with potential for error. Since mitochondrial DNA is passed along from a mother to her children, relatives sharing a maternal bloodline will have the same profile. And chemical treatments like peroxide degrade and weaken the DNA.

The biggest misconception around forensic evidence, Morgan argues, is that it's irrefutable. She points to the case of Englishman Barri White as an example of how the fallibility of forensic evidence can result in a devastating miscarriage of justice. Convicted of murder, in part because of the misinterpretation of the significance of metallic particles found on the passenger seat of his codefendant's van and also on the victim's skirt, he spent six years in prison. Later, the conviction was overturned and White was freed.

Across the Atlantic, human error comes with an even heavier price. An FBI report in 2015 revealed that over 90 percent of microscopic hair analyses were found to contain erroneous statements in the US.

Of the 500 cases reviewed by the FBI that year, at least 35 defendants had received the death penalty and nine had already been executed. "Forensic science is able to provide powerful evidence, but it has to be interpreted correctly," says Morgan. To place all of our trust in it would be criminal.

DEAD ENDS

by Harriet Fitch Little

As the communist revolution gained pace in 1920s China, women bobbed their hair short as a sign of liberation. It was a high-risk move: Those sporting the cut were easily identifiable as rebel forces, and many were executed. This was not the first time in China that having the wrong haircut had proved deadly. From the 17th to the early 20th century, men were obliged to wear their hair in a distinctive style known as the *queue*: totally shaved at the front, and pulled together in a long braid at the back. Introduced by the Manchu people—the conquering force that charged into China in 1618 and established the 250-year Qing dynasty—the hairstyle was a marker of servitude imposed on everyone who fell under their domain, even the Korean king. The punishment for non-compliance was execution or, as a popular slogan summarized it: "Keep your hair and lose your head, or keep your head and cut your hair." In a society where a full head of hair was a badge of honor, class and filial piety, many Hans initially chose to die rather than cut their locks. And yet, as with all fashions, the queue was quickly normalized in Qing society—to the point where the half-shaved, half-braided look itself became a mark of high social standing by the 19th century. The queue's end was less dramatic than its beginning. With wealthy Chinese merchants increasingly traveling to Europe and America, the hairstyle that had signaled first servitude and then superiority developed a new context: a point of ridicule for racist foreigners. Children pulled men's braids, and cartoonists used them to characterize the Chinese as feminine. Reformers pushing for a more modern China decided that the by-now-traditional style had to go.

Spitting Hairs

It's a squeamish moment, finding a hair that doesn't belong to you snaking through your spaghetti— one that usually warrants a swift return of the plate to the restaurant kitchen, or profuse apologies from whichever family member's 'do matches the length and color of the sample. In her seminal book, *Purity and Danger*, anthropologist Mary Douglas outlines the cultural codes that create this aversion. As "matter out of place," that stray hair symbolizes a disruption to our established order. We are shocked to see the pedestrian become perverse.

Yet our aversion to a single strand does seem misplaced given that human hair is added to many commercially baked goods in the form of an amino acid called L-Cysteine. While this is not the only surprising ingredient that lurks in our favorite foods— some artificial treats owe their fragrant vanilla flavoring to the pungent castoreum that is secreted under the tail of beavers—it's still a tough one to swallow. Reportedly harvested from barbershops and hair salons in China, the hair is dissolved in acid to isolate the L-Cysteine. From there, it's shipped off to commercial producers who rely on it to prolong the shelf life and enhance the salty flavor of breads, bagels and breakfast pastries. Fast food chains all rely on the additive, although some claim to use a synthetic variation.

Do we need to worry? Hair is made from a dense protein called keratin, a key structural material also found in skin and nails, as well as in hooves, claws and horns. The FDA doesn't quantify the number of hairs that would need to be swallowed to create a health hazard, although consuming a full head's worth could cause a painful hairball to form in the stomach. And L-Cysteine is only one tiny amino acid in the grand scheme of things—not actual hair. In other words, the most hair-raising side effect is the very thought of those strays being swept up in the first place. Bon appétit.

"Being a milliner is akin to being a bartender or a shrink," says Ellen Christine, a New York-based hat-maker whose creations have graced the glossy heads of some of the world's most illustrious women. With 36 years of experience and a doctorate in costume design to her name, Christine crafts headpieces that artfully blend fantasy with practicality. Here, the grand dame shares her advice for good hat etiquette—and explains the psychological benefits of wearing one.

What's the most important thing to consider when buying a hat? Remember that a hat is meant to frame your face and highlight your features, especially your eyes. The most important thing about wearing a hat is making people look directly at your face when they're speaking to you, not at the hat.

How do you choose the right hat for an occasion? Different hats are intended for different situations. If we're talking about church, it should be a hat that allows you to kiss someone hello, receive communion without bobbing feathers into the priest's hand and it should be a little bit chic. The Kentucky Derby requires something phantasmagorical. Get away from the plastic horses and goo-ga—instead it should be colorful, floral and contain elements of brightness, happiness and joyfulness. Hats for the Derby can be playful and fun without being plastic.

Do you match the hat to the clothes or vice versa? Start from the head down. Don't worry about your outfit so much because it's not the '60s—we're not trying to make you look like a bridesmaid. If you start with the hat it'll be much easier for you to coordinate the ensemble. After all, getting dressed is about how *you* look, not how the dress or the jewelry looks.

Should a hat be approached as an investment piece? I believe that a hat should be timeless. It shouldn't be stuck in a moment or a fashion trend, but rather create a world unto itself. It'll be something that you could wear now and in 10 years—perhaps, if your face hasn't completely fallen and you can still wear the same style.

What do we gain from wearing hats? I never think of hats as being restrictive. Rather, I think of them as being a freeing element. Everyone has so many different personalities inside themselves and hats allow us to extract and show those personalities without becoming too extreme.

How to Wear a Hat

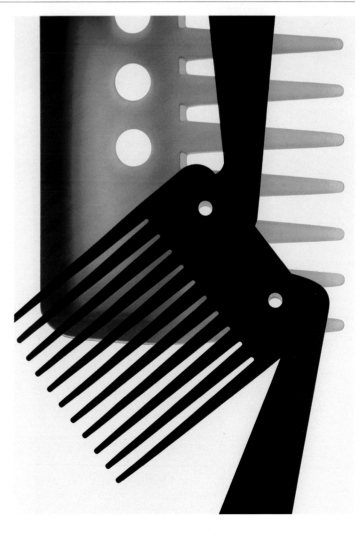

HOLY HAIR
by Harriet Fitch Little

The veneration of relics is one thing many religions can agree on. From Buddha's tooth in Sri Lanka to St. Anthony's tongue in Italy, the faithful flock to witness—and worship—the bodily remains of holy figures, through which the grace of some higher power is believed to flow. Hair has always been one of the more abundant relics: It is easily harvested and a person generally has a lot of it, a fact which prevents awkward questions arising about authenticity. (In the Middle Ages, it emerged that a dozen different churches claimed to be in possession of Jesus Christ's foreskin.) Hair is also one of the few relics that has retained its currency in secular circles. In the Victorian era, preserving the hair of loved ones became a popular pursuit: Families would weave their tresses into mourning wreaths. Nowadays we have more high-tech ways of remembering our dearly departed, but the veneration of hair has once more shifted shape—this time into the lucrative celebrity memorabilia market. At online auctions, famous hair can (and frequently does) sell for upwards of $100,000. Its valuation follows a similar logic to that of art: The death of its maker ups the value, as does any connection to an important biographical event. So, just as Van Gogh's most famous self-portrait is the one he painted after cutting off his ear, Michael Jackson's most prized hair clippings are those collected after he accidentally caught on fire when filming a Pepsi commercial in 1984. Before rolling your eyes at the worship of celebrities in place of saints, spare a thought for the researchers who have reaped the benefits of this unusual hobby. Without the ghoulish fans who snipped Beethoven's hair as he lay on his deathbed, 21st-century scientists would never have been able to test the great composer's locks and reach the intriguing conclusion that he died of lead poisoning.

The deep-rooted history of hair removal.

Excessive Growth

Hair removal is a painful pillar of the 21st-century beauty routine. Yet our discomfort pales into insignificance next to the elaborate rituals practiced by our forebears. From the cavemen who used sharply whittled stones to scrape off facial hair to the elegant courtiers of the Elizabethan era who followed the queen's fondness for a high forehead by applying bandages soaked in ammonia and vinegar to their brows, hair—or the lack thereof—has always been an obsession.

Picture an ancient Egyptian and it's most likely to be Cleopatra, with her sleek black bob. Underneath it, though, she was bald; like most of her contemporaries, the queen shaved her head and then affixed an immaculate and perfumed wig made from human hair. And it wasn't just hair on the head that was removed. Body hair was imbued with shameful connotations; it was considered unclean and common by upper class Egyptians who pioneered mechanisms of removing it that live on today. Women mixed up homemade sugar and beeswax-based waxes to strip hair from their entire bodies, while male priests plucked out their eyelashes and eyebrows with rudimentary tweezers made from seashells. Facial hair was occasionally sported by pharaohs but

even that was a facade—the plaited beard was a metallic accessory attached to a smoothly shaven face.

In the Roman Empire, beards slipped even further in public opinion; they were a marker of slavery, servitude and barbarity. The Roman upper class's fetishization of hairlessness can be seen in the numerous nude statues which show not a trace of pubic hair on either sex. Religious significance was also attached to the ritualistic removal of hair—a young man's first shave was a much-anticipated ceremonial event attended by friends and family, after which the whiskers were housed in a consecrated box. From then on, patricians employed the help of a personal barber while the less well-off maintained respectability at local barbershops.

Despite Europe's enduring obsession with hair removal, it wasn't until the 18th century that primitive bronze razors were replaced with a more sophisticated, and less hazardous, model. Alongside a book titled *The Art of Shaving Oneself*, Parisian barber Jean-Jacques Perret invented a blade that was partially enclosed by a wooden sleeve. A century later, an American businessman by the name of King Camp Gillette patented a razor with a T-shaped handle and disposable blade. Suddenly, shav-

ing had become safe, easy and affordable to all.

Changing fashions ushered in revealing clothes that placed a spotlight on women's body hair again. In the early 20th century, sleeveless evening gowns forced women to confront their underarms. By the 1940s, a shortage of silk and nylon during World War II, coupled with rising hemlines, had compelled bare-legged women to consider their leg hair, too. In the ensuing decades, an abundance of hair removal products burst on to the market, from do-it-yourself depilatory creams and wax strips to electrolysis and, later, lasers.

Five thousand years after the ancient Egyptians, our equipment is more sophisticated but our distaste for unregulated body hair seems the same. Yet there have been recent moves to combat this societal obsession, from Instagram accounts celebrating women's natural body hair to female celebrities sharing pictures of their underarm growth. Fashion brands have started to take note—Swedish label & Other Stories ran a 2015 campaign featuring models with unshaved armpits. After millennia of technological innovation, perhaps we'll end up back where we started: hairy and happy about it.

David Byrne

The musical polymath talks fame and failure.

It would be a mistake to pigeon-hole David Byrne. Best known as lead singer and principal songwriter of Talking Heads, the 66-year-old resists categorization—with pleasure. He is an Oscar-winning film composer, a collaborator with Robert Wilson and Fatboy Slim, a bike-rack designer, and, more recently, creator of a virtual reality piece inspired by neuroscience research. In his spare time, he curates the website Reasons to Be Cheerful, a repository for positive things happening around the world that can be reproduced elsewhere. In March, he released *American Utopia*, his first solo album in 14 years. It has since taken him on a massive international tour, during which he is surely discovering more ideas to fuel his optimism. Before he embarked, Byrne sat down in New York City to discuss a heady array of topics, from the need to treat audiences intelligently to the benefits of leaving certain jobs, even if you do the work well.

You've said that the body understands music before the head does. Do you pay attention to how crowds move while you play? You can't see the whole audience, but you can see enough to tell if they're physically engaged. I tend to feel that people perceive sound and its structure as a metaphor for something else, something beyond music. I think that's largely unconscious, and that's where some of the enjoyment comes from; it implies a way of organiz-ing things socially or perceptually, and it does it without language. People know what music feels like. They know if they like it, but they don't analyze why.

How smart are audiences? They're as smart as the way you treat them. Treat them with respect, intelligence and empathy, and they respond in kind. Treat them as passive receivers of songs that they know—the hits that trigger instant enjoyment—and they'll regress to being that kind of consumer as opposed to being more engaged. I'll pander up to a point, but audiences don't want that either. They might think they do, but they actually want surprises as well.

How does music differ from other art forms? In the late '70s and early '80s, many visual artists went on to incredible continued success, whereas only a handful of musicians did. Maybe it's because you can accept visual art very quickly and see it over and over again. Music is time-based; you have to sit through it. That era's music was often somewhat aggressive, so it's not like you could do anything but sit through it, whereas with art you can look at it and have a conversation at the same time. Music can be emotionally engaging background sound and also something you stop and listen to with your full attention. You have options with how you want to take it in.

Do you have any pre-show rituals? I make ginger tea with lemon and honey, sometimes turmeric—the ingredients are on the rider! It becomes a ritual because I make it myself: I peel the ginger, chop it, let it steep. It takes at least 10 minutes, taking me outside of thinking about what's about to happen.

Your career has been so varied. Have you ever felt that an endeavor just wasn't quite right for you, or had something not work out the way you had planned it? Failure is a luxury I had early with Talking Heads as well as with some of my own stuff. You did something that didn't work in front of 30 people and you could junk it. It was no big deal. I wonder whether, now that everything can get disseminated so quickly, the idea of being able to fail publicly and learn from it is being squashed. The internet makes it harder for people to fail because they know that whatever they do might get out. The audience needs to accept that not everything that everyone does is going to be successful; they might have bad ideas sometimes.

I had a small record label for many years called Luaka Bop. It still exists, but although I could run the business, that wasn't the best use of my time. I realized that my skills might be better utilized doing things that other people can't do, and that, even though I could handle what I was doing, there were other people who could do it better than I could. Just because you can do something doesn't mean that's what you should be doing.

"The mind is a soft boiled potato," sings David Byrne on his new album. As the lyric suggests, Byrne's own brain is often powered by sideways tangents.

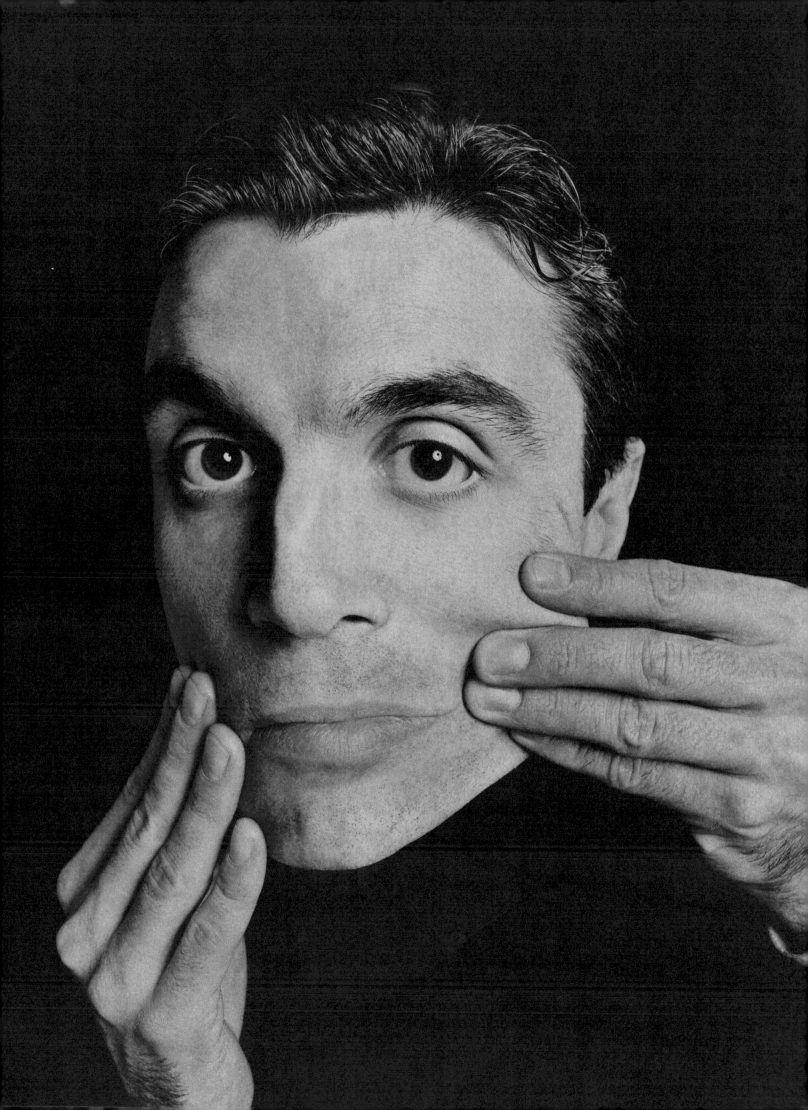

Why painters paint themselves.

PIP USHER

By Oneself

Perhaps what moves us when we look at self-portraiture is its inherent tension. It feels intimate, and yet we are aware that the composition has been carefully engineered for public consumption.

If eyes are the window to the soul, then what can we learn from a self-portrait? Take Frida Kahlo, perhaps the world's most iconic self-portraitist. Much of her enduring legacy, as explored in London's Victoria & Albert Museum's summer exhibition, *Frida Kahlo: Making Her Self Up*, remains centered around the vivid visual power of her person as told through her self-portraits. What do we uncover of Kahlo through them? "In Frida's case, she was not thinking of becoming famous when she was painting herself," says Hilda Trujillo, director of both the Frida Kahlo Museum and the Anahuacalli Museum in Mexico City.

As Trujillo points out, the first time that Kahlo recreated her own image was for love: When imploring a boyfriend "not to forget about her," she sent him a beautiful painting of her visage. Shortly after divorcing fellow artist Diego Rivera, she created a bleak painting that showed her shorn of hair and dressed (uncharacteristically) in dark menswear. Her chronic physical pain proved another enduring theme: "Frida knew how to transform pain and adversity into a work of art," says Trujillo. "She created honest and original images of herself that helped her to live her life transcending her physical obstacle."

Several decades later, American photographer Nan Goldin also began turning her deepest feelings and darkest moments into art. *The Ballad of Sexual Dependency*—a diaristic series of photos taken in Boston, Berlin and New York throughout the '70s and '80s—laid Goldin and her "tribe" bare. Drug use, sexual interludes and domestic abuse punctuated their lives as they searched for intimacy. In her most famous self-portrait, Goldin stares straight into the camera—wearing curly hair, a pearl necklace, and two swollen black eyes inflicted upon her by a lover. "Nan One Month After Being Battered," the caption reads.

Now that technology has placed a camera in all our hands, self-portraits have become a pedestrian part of daily life. It's not the raw agony of Kahlo or the gritty immediacy of Goldin that has shaped selfie culture, though. Instead, we look to Andy Warhol, whose own stylized self-portraits featured brightly colored heads floating across a dark canvas—like Instagram shots with a few too many filters applied. "I am a deeply superficial person," he once said. His attitude toward art proved prescient of things to come.

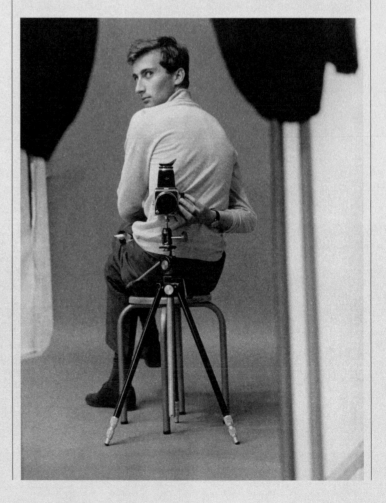

Photograph: Jeanloup Sieff

ASHER ROSS

On the Fly

Though a summer bother, the humble fruit fly is science's greatest muse.

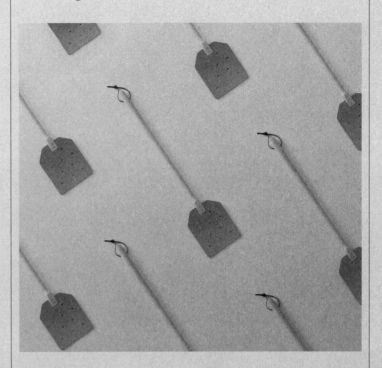

In the frigid New York winter of 1910, experimental biologist Thomas Hunt Morgan etherized a family of fruit flies and began sorting through their sleeping forms. After a while he saw something unusual—a fly with white eyes.

In all his time studying *Drosophila melanogaster*, Morgan had seen only red eyes, or more specifically, red compounds with 760 individual lenses. What confronted him now was a rare genetic mutant. He bred the fly, eventually yielding a cohort with those same ghostly features. His experiment established the material basis of heredity in the chromosome, providing an essential "How?" that had been missing from Darwin's theory of evolution.

It also earned Morgan the Nobel Prize, and made the fruit fly the sine qua non of 20th-century biological research. Subsequent work on *Drosophila* has yielded five additional Nobel Prizes, and expanded our understanding of disease, memory, addiction, the circadian rhythm and the aging process itself. Untold millions of fruit flies have been sacrificed at the altar of human knowledge.

We should love them for this, but our revulsion remains: Flies have an unshakeable association with decay and death. It's awful to lift a peach only to see its underside infested with tiny, squirming dots. Emily Dickinson imagined a fly buzzing while she died in order to signify the absence of God. David Cronenberg turned Jeff Goldblum into one in a 1986 horror film.

It's true that flies seek out decay in order to live. But few species testify to life's desire for continuance so persistently. *Drosophila* live a mad-dash existence, sprinting through birth, courtship, reproduction and death in roughly 30 days. This extraordinary pace is part of what makes them so indispensable to science, allowing researchers to observe several generations quickly and on the cheap. We now know that fruit flies share 60 percent of our own genetic material, and present analogues for three-quarters of all human disease. They are squirming under microscopes all over the world as you read this.

And yet homes are not laboratories, and common sense tells us to rid ourselves of these unwelcome guests. But it may be useful, for our sanity at least, to recognize that these invaders are tokens of the same procreative rush that created our own species. The humble fruit fly is a household reminder of how little we know and how far we've come. It's worth contemplating as one reaches for the swatter.

HOW TO KILL A FLY
by Asher Ross

Many of us agree that the flies in the lab must stay and that the ones buzzing around the fruit bowl must go. But how to get rid of them? Fruit flies' evasive capacities have evolved to an exquisite degree. One study at the California Institute of Technology found that they can instantaneously respond to looming shadows, adjusting their flight paths in a tenth of a second. The researchers, aiming for practicality rather than another *Drosophila* Nobel, advise us to ignore the fly's starting position in favor of a spot slightly in front of it. The idea is to anticipate the fly's maneuver. Lisa Dennison, a former fruit fly researcher at University of California, Berkeley, recommends a craftier approach. "They're very attracted to vinegar or juice. Apple juice is best because it doesn't stink up the house. Pour some into a small, open container and then add some dish soap to break the surface tension. They fall in, sink and drown." Asked if she thought this might be a cruel end to a brief life, Dennison offered a lovely speculation. "Fruit flies have taste neurons not only on their proboscis, but also on their legs. Whenever they land, they're tasting it right away. This way, before drowning, they're experiencing fruit fly heaven for one brief moment."

Cult Rooms

Matisse's cutouts were dismissed by contemporaries as a childish indulgence. Today, many consider them his masterpiece.

Old, ill and bedridden in Nice, Matisse staged a surprise final act.

Henri Matisse chose his final residence well. The Palais Regina in Nice had been built for Queen Victoria in 1897. It featured electronic elevators, central heating and croquet lawns—plus sea views from the 80 rooms needed to accommodate the entourage of the planet's most powerful woman.

Nice receives 300 glorious days of sun per year and as the sun flooded Matisse's bedroom, the northerner could shove open his louvered shutters to reveal a living canvas: azure seas, bronzed limbs, green palms that swish-swished like an enlivened brush against a burnished yellow sun. Simple colors, simple life.

The resulting work was far removed from the nutty fauvism of his formative years. Now he was like a child let loose with tubs of primary colors. Monochrome blue nudes and color-blocked fronds climbed his bedroom walls.

Picasso would call in to needle his older rival; the fiery Catalan poked the bourgeois Frenchman toward greater creativity. The two embodied the interwar spirit by collaborating on stage sets for the Ballets Russes in Monte Carlo. (This being the French Riviera, Coco Chanel stitched the ballet costumes, while Jean Cocteau designed the posters.) Matisse contributed bold cutouts of colored paper that he pinned directly onto the prima ballerina.

But change was coming. While Matisse was visiting Paris in the spring of 1940, Nazi hordes fell upon the city. He fled back to Nice, only to be diagnosed with abdominal cancer. The wartime surgery left him bound to either his bed or a wheelchair.

Yet slowly, strangely, avant-garde stardust sprang from his aged hands. He could still grasp a long cane, with a paintbrush tacked on the end, which he used to swoosh linear shapes on his remaining bare walls. "Work cures everything," he once claimed. Like a wheelchair general, he chivvied on teams of assistants who gouached reams of paper. Cutting was easier than painting, and so the shapes were snipped, arranged and colla-ged. They formed a circus of animated figures for a limited edition art tome named *Jazz*. At age 74 he had the confidence to embark on an unexpected final act—a "second life" as he gratefully called it. In 1943, Allied bombs rained down on Nice's rail depot near the Palais Regina. Matisse fled once more, this time to the hilltop town of Vence. A young nurse, Monique Bourgeois, tended to him by night and posed by day. She later entered the local convent and told him of plans by Dominican monks to construct a new chapel in Vence. She asked Matisse to help. He not only offered to design the entire structure but to pay for it as well.

Matisse's atheism horrified the Catholic clergy, and Picasso purportedly recommended that he decorate a brothel instead. Yet, in a piece of cosmic alignment, the dimensions of his apartment back in Nice followed the chapel's floor plan. This allowed him to design what he would later attest was his "masterpiece" from the comfort of his bed, or as he wheeled across the Palais Regina's parquet.

Using a lump of charcoal attached to a bamboo pole he sketched the chapel's Passion of Christ mural. Ever the perfectionist, he designed the holy water bowls and priests' garments too. The final effect is light-filled and expansive, like the view from his apartment windows in Nice.

Still more works came from his Palais Regina years. His vast cutout gouaches, "drawing with scissors" as he called it, included *Blue Nude IV* in 1952. As his body hibernated, the spirit reverted to youth. His last piece was a portrait of his final muse, Lydia Delectorskaya, drawn on plain paper with a ballpoint pen. The artist passed away at 84, his bedroom walls overtaken by a technicolor jungle of figures and leaves. Matisse was interred in the cemetery of the Monastère Notre Dame de Cimiez, near both the Palais Regina and Musée Matisse. Schoolchildren have peppered his grave with their own drawings. As Matisse would have wanted, it marks a naive return to a playful youth.

The Joy of Nightwalking

While the city sleeps, our senses come to life.

In nearly all major cities, the metro system closes during the darkest hours of the night. Though that time is often used for cleaning and repairs, this shutting down may be an unconscious nod to the night's unique rhythms—as if the tracks themselves might change in the midnight hours, the day's trains not designed to traverse them. Of course, there are taxis and night buses, but when traveling in the dark, walking should be our preferred mode of transportation.

Nightwalking—choosing to perambulate after businesses have shut down and most people are asleep—is rebellious. It serves few, if any, obvious purposes, and that deliberate purposelessness is precisely what makes it seem unacceptable. In a world dominated by crisp images, products designed for ultra-specific uses, overscheduling, and statistical analyses that compartmentalize the world into increasingly defined categories, the out-of-focus night is swaddled by darkness and infused with aimlessness.

That the illumination of the urban environment began during the Enlightenment is unsurprising; it reflects the era's worship of reason and clarity. Such artificial brightness makes the line between night and day more indistinguishable—to our detriment. As "leisure time" becomes unabashedly consumed by answering work emails, and "nightlife" does not introduce alternative ways of being but just new ways to consume, we must consider what is lost as the darkness vanishes.

The daily commute, with its visual monotony of chain stores and other familiar sights, mollifies us through repetition. Nightwalking, on the other hand, requires heightened alertness. As the city changes appearance, new landmarks arise and the darkness becomes pregnant with unknown possibilities. It opens up a space of potential. In its purest sense, nightwalking provides choices—choices not available when the demands of commerce and traffic and countless other needs delimit our every move. At night, however, the empty road yields to the uninhibited peripatetic. As Nick Dunn writes in *Dark Matters: A Manifesto for the Nocturnal City*, this second side of the metropolis "appears somehow more porous; the shadowplay across its edifices is rich, deep and gelatinous. In addition, and perhaps of greater significance, it fosters a different way of thinking. In an age of hyper-visibility, encountering anything genuinely new seems incredibly remote, weirdly distanced from us yet at the same time ever-present and depthless."

Architecture takes on new forms as the entirety of even the simplest buildings appear consumed by thick blackness. Details discernible during the day vanish as the edges of structures are swallowed into the ether. With our eyes less focused, other senses become heightened. Contours of the city otherwise inaudible or eluding our nostrils are made apparent, creating new cartographies.

The haze allows a shedding of identity, too. On a daily basis, we are followed by surveillance cameras, have our online activity monitored and voluntarily give more access to the world than is demanded. On social media, for example, friends and strangers alike follow our moves by locations we tag in our social posts. Conversely, at night, people—if they are visible at all—do not even appear as individuals but mere shapes, sometimes just human-like outlines. This purging of identity allows for countless freedoms—from social conventions, ideological impositions, personal commitments. It fulfills what French philosopher and literary theorist Maurice Blanchot asserted as "the right to disappear." As Dunn puts it: "The idea of being absent, to really embrace 'lack' of interference, seems like a surreal, utopian construct. Deliberately opting out of 24/7 availability, and therefore conventionally accepted accountability in the twenty-first century is a choice, albeit a very particular one."

Societies that value clarity, exposure, and constant presence often forget the potential of the ephemeral and the inexplicable. They also forget the benefits of contemplation and suggestion, gravitating toward sureness and the well-defined. Yet there is comfort to be found in discomfort, and beauty in the void. As Matthew Beaumont writes in *Nightwalking: A Nocturnal History of London*, the act is "extravagant" in an etymological sense, meaning that it involves "wandering beyond bounds, both geographical and social." From the Latin *vagari*, meaning "to wander," these nighttime vagabonds carve uncharted paths.

During the day, homes and other interiors can serve as refuge from the outside cacophony. At night, they tend to prove even more comforting. But when viewed from the street in the dark, these rooms appear like hermetically sealed cells, the window-framed lights putting those inside on display. Take Edward Hopper's *Nighthawks*, with its inhabitants trapped and brooding in a diner; they no doubt know there isn't a door through which they might escape. Ask yourself: Would you choose to be one of Hopper's immobile characters, sealed in for the night, or would you rather cavort freely, like Anita Ekberg in *La Dolce Vita*, wading into fountains and other spaces to which access is prohibited when the sun shines overhead, the unboundedness letting you dream with eyes open?

When Charles Dickens killed off a character he loved, he would walk the streets until dawn as a form of catharsis.

Find a willing partner, and go down (and across) on this euphemistic puzzle. No blushing.

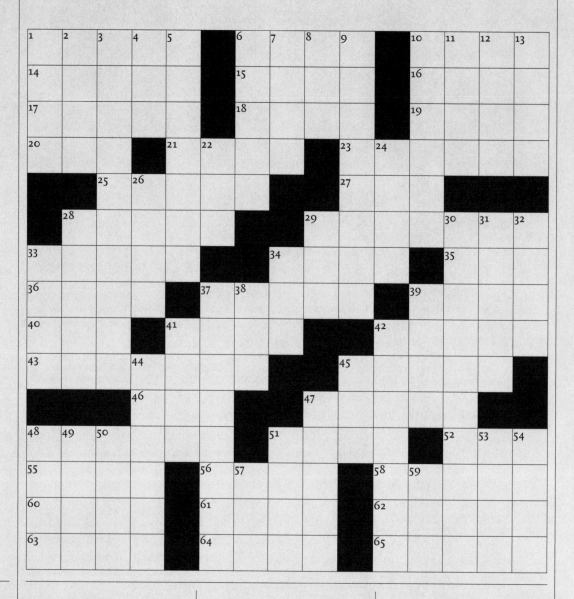

MOLLY YOUNG

Crossword

ACROSS

1. *The official tally of points in a game or sport
6. Monty Python member Idle
10. *Type of hairdo or rug
14. Purple flowering plant in the pea family
15. Long ride?
16. Wedding dress element, often
17. To-do list entries
18. Stroke of luck
19. Leo Tolstoy's Karenina
20. John Steinbeck's "Of Mice and ___"
21. Flying saucers
23. Gushing geothermal spout
25. *Fastener with a helical ridge
27. Hearty brown bread
28. Form of certain cosmetic products (or desserts)
29. African mammal known for standing on its hind legs
33. Pay attention
34. Give some lip
35. The utmost degree
36. Attract
37. Complies
39. Aristocratic sport on horseback
40. Grow older
41. Zenith
42. Until 1999, the last European colony in Asia
43. *1971 T.Rex single
45. Toils
46. Two en español
47. Cake or cookie tidbit
48. Old-style internet connections
51. Methods
52. Spoiled, as in milk
55. Operatic solo
56. Embattled ridesharing app
58. Stow away
60. Like André the Giant
61. Only
62. Eroded
63. Pipe joints shaped like right angles
64. Observes
65. Took medicine

DOWN

1. Slender
2. Adorable
3. A poorly-kept confidence
4. Part of a volcano or a wine glass
5. Guarantees
6. Pasta shape
7. Rivers in Mexico
8. "As I see it," in a text message.
9. *Lawmaking group
10. "Reign in Blood" thrash metal band
11. Danish fairy tale writer ___ Christian Andersen
12. Teen spots?
13. Equipment
22. Price of entry
24. Ogles
26. Hint
28. Take advantage of
29. Orson Welles and Salvador Dalí birthday month
30. *What you may do to remove mud from your shoes
31. Geographical reference book
32. You, in the Bible
33. Physical symbol of nationhood
34. The starred clues are all ways to say this
37. Marsupials that "play dead"
38. London's Big ___
39. Chicken ____ sandwich
41. Smallest smidgen
42. Like some 1980s hairstyles
44. Exemplars
45. Sardonic
47. Concerns
48. *Pal
49. Like some vaccines and exams
50. Herb commonly served with salmon
51. 1973 Sydney Pollack film "The Way We ___"
53. Unshackled
54. Resist
57. Something to keep out of your bonnet
59. Chinese for "path"

New York stylist *Vaughn Acord* has been cutting hair for nearly four decades. He's also spent innumerable hours in swiveling seats, having worked as a model in his youth. For *Kinfolk*, Acord shares his top tips for good salon etiquette—and explains why the client-stylist relationship runs far deeper than talking about holiday plans.

Vaughn Acord

When you arrive at the salon, remember to be patient. Your stylist may be running a few minutes behind with another client who's having a hard time personally. As in the rest of life, you never know what someone is going through. There is an intimacy between stylist and client—we have our hands on your hair, and we're working to give you a look that brings you confidence—but that intimacy has to come naturally. I like to begin with basic conversation starters and see how things evolve throughout the appointment and throughout all of our appointments. A stylist-client conversation can be as natural as any other conversation, just with more hair involved. And if you aren't in a chatty mood once you get to the chair, that's okay too. Stylists won't take silence for rudeness. Sometimes people wonder where they should look during an appointment. Feel free to sit back and shut your eyes during your shampoo— the scalp massage feels great, so enjoy it. When we're cutting your hair you can make eye contact in the mirror— we're concentrating but can pause. I also have some clients who just look at themselves in the mirror all appointment and that's fine too—whatever works for you. Don't sit there with your hot drink going cold—you're supposed to enjoy it. Just give your stylist a heads up that you are going to move. We are wielding scissors and razors after all.

RAINS

Drip, drip, drip.

rains.com

Stockists

ACNE STUDIOS
acnestudios.com

ALTALEN
altalen.it

ANDERSON & SHEPPARD
anderson-sheppard.co.uk

A.P.C.
apc.fr

BURBERRY
burberry.com

CALVIN KLEIN
calvinklein.com

CÉDRIC CHARLIER
cedriccharlier.com

CÉLINE
celine.com

CHIN MENSWEAR
chinmenswear.net

COMME DES GARÇONS
comme-des-garcons.com

CORNELIA WEBB
corneliawebb.com

CORNELIANI
corneliani.com

COS
cosstores.com

ERIKA CAVALLINI
erikacavallini.com

ERMENEGILDO ZEGNA
zegna.com

FENDI
fendi.com

FRAMA
framacph.com

GABRIELE COLANGELO
gabrielecolangelo.com

GEORGE CLEVERLEY
georgecleverley.com

GIEVES & HAWKES
gievesandhawkes.com

GOODS BY GOODHOOD
goodhoodstore.com

JW ANDERSON
j-w-anderson.com

JACQUEMUS
jacquemus.com

KENZO
kenzo.com

KRIZIA
krizia.it

LA BAGAGERIE
labagagerie.com

LANVIN
lanvin.com

LEMAIRE
lemaire.fr

LINDBERG
lindberg.com

MACKINTOSH
mackintosh.com

MADEMOISELLE CHAPEAUX
mademoisellechapeaux.com

MAISON TRACLET
chapellerie-traclet.com

MARGARET HOWELL
margarethowell.co.uk

MARSET
marset.com

MASHA MA
masha-ma.com

MERCHANT ARCHIVE
merchantarchive.com

MOLLY GODDARD
mollygoddard.com

MUUTO
muuto.com

MYKITA
mykita.com

OFF-WHITE
off—white.com

PANTHERELLA
pantherella.com

PAULA KNORR
paulaknorr.uk

POMELLATO
pomellato.com

PRINGLE OF SCOTLAND
pringlescotland.com

RAINS
rains.com

REJINA PYO
rejinapyo.com

ROCHAS
rochas.com

ROLEX
rolex.com

SANDRO PARIS
sandro-paris.com

SANTONI BY MARCO ZANINI
santonishoes.com

SHUSHU/TONG
shushutongstudio.com

SKIIM
skiim-london.com

SUNSPEL
sunspel.com

THE DIRTY INC.
thedirtyinc.com

THE LINE
theline.com

TOGA ARCHIVES
toga.jp

VIEN
vien.it

XANDER ZHOU
xanderzhou.com

YMC
youmustcreate.com

YUUL YIE
yuulyieshop.com

ISSUE 28

Credits

COVER
Photographer
Annie Lai
Stylist
Kingsley Tao
Hair
Hirokazu Endo
Makeup
Phebe Wu
Model
Daniel Ward-Thomas
at IMG Models

Location
Sorrento, Italy

Daniel wears a shirt by
JW Anderson, a suit by
Chin Menswear, a tie by
Lanvin, belt by Margaret
Howell and a necklace by
Goods by Goodhood

P. 27
Brendan wears a jacket by
COS, a top by Sunspel and
trousers by Boglioli

P. 40
Lauren wears a top by COS
and her own jewelry

P. 66 — 77
Casting
Sarah Bunter
Hair
Shukeel Murtaza using Sam
McKnight
Makeup
Victoria Bond using Sisley
Models
Raith Clarke at Supa Model
Management and *Betty
Adewole* at IMG Models

P. 67
Betty wears a dress by
Shushu/Tong

P. 88 — 103
Casting
Sarah Bunter
Hair
Hirokazu Endo
Makeup
Phebe Wu
Models
Daniel Ward-Thomas at
IMG Models and *Layla
Ong* at WOMEN Model
Management

P. 89
Layla wears a vest by Toga
Archives, a jacket, skirt and
shoes by Masha Ma, a hat
by Off White and earrings
by Paula Knorr.

P. 101
Daniel wears Margaret
Howell head-to-toe.

P. 108
Photograph: Reporters
Associati & Archivi/
Mondadori Portfolio/Getty
Images

P. 126 — 135
Hair
Christos Vourlis
Makeup
Maria Olsson
Model
Veronika Vasilyeva at
Next Models

P. 136 — 147
Stylist's Assistant
Marta Mankiewicz

P. 148
This article is an abridged
and edited excerpt from
Naïm: A Brush with History
(Darya Press, Beirut 2013),
republished with the
kind permission of its
author *Carole Corm* and
Darya Press

P. 152
Coat by Burberry, dress by
JW Anderson and shoes by
COS

P. 154
Coat by Burberry and dress
by JW Anderson

P. 156
Dress by JW Anderson and
shoes by COS

P. 157
Top by COS, jacket and skirt
by Cédric Charlier

P. 158
Top is stylist's own

P. 159 — 160
Coat by Mackintosh

P. 182
Photograph: Gjon Mili//
Time Life Pictures/Getty
Images

Special Thanks:
James Smith
Jonathan Demers at Toronto
Reference Library
Eiman Zarrug
Secondo Pensiero
The Graham Foundation
Triennale Milano